COACHING FOR MULTILINGUAL EXCELLENCE

DEDICATION

To my loved ones: Luis Mauricio, Hollis, Danica, and Pacman.

To the Margarita Calderón & Associates team: Lisa Tartaglia, Hector Montenegro, Leticia Trower, Karen Solis, Lillian Ardell, Cristina Zakis, Giulianna J. Lewis, Alyson Reilly, Rebecca Upchurch, Joanne Marino, Guadalupe Espino, Heather Cox, Nanci Esparza, and April Vazquez.

COACHING FOR MULTILINGUAL EXCELLENCE

Strategies for **Vocabulary, Reading,** and **Writing Across Disciplines**

Margarita Espino
CALDERÓN

FOR INFORMATION

Corwin
A SAGE Company
2455 Teller Road
Thousand Oaks, California 91320
(800) 233-9936
www.corwin.com

SAGE Publications Ltd.
1 Oliver's Yard
55 City Road
London EC1Y 1SP
United Kingdom

SAGE Publications India Pvt. Ltd.
Unit No 323-333, Third Floor, F-Block
International Trade Tower Nehru Place
New Delhi 110 019
India

SAGE Publications Asia-Pacific Pte. Ltd.
18 Cross Street #10-10/11/12
China Square Central
Singapore 048423

Vice President and
 Editorial Director: Monica Eckman
Acquisitions Editor: Megan Bedell
Content Development
 Editor: Mia Rodriguez
Content Development
 Manager: Lucas Schleicher
Senior Editorial Assistant: Natalie Delpino
Production Editor: Tori Mirsadjadi
Copy Editor: Melinda Masson
Typesetter: C&M Digitals (P) Ltd.
Cover Designer: Gail Buschman
Marketing Manager: Melissa Duclos

Printed in the United States of America

Library of Congress Cataloging-in-Publication Data

Names: Calderón, Margarita, author.

Title: Coaching for multilingual excellence : strategies for vocabulary, reading, and writing across disciplines / Margarita Espino Calderón.

Description: Thousand Oaks, California : Corwin, 2025. | Includes bibliographical references and index.

Identifiers: LCCN 2024028865 | ISBN 9781071936429 (paperback) | ISBN 9781071936436 (epub) | ISBN 9781071936443 (epub) | ISBN 9781071936467 (pdf)

Subjects: LCSH: Multilingual education—United States. | Linguistic minorities—Education—United States. | Language arts—Social aspects—United States. | English language—Study and teaching—United States—Foreign speakers. | Mentoring in education—United States.

Classification: LCC LC3731 .C2895 2025 | DDC 370.117/50973—dc23/eng/20240729

LC record available at https://lccn.loc.gov/2024028865

This book is printed on acid-free paper.

SUSTAINABLE FORESTRY INITIATIVE Certified Sourcing www.sfiprogram.org SFI-01028

24 25 26 27 28 10 9 8 7 6 5 4 3 2 1

Contents

Chapter 2. What Do Instructional Coaches Need to Know to Coach Teachers With Multilingual Learners?   47

Chapter 3. Coaching Reading Teaching and Learning — 73

Website Contents

To download the above tools and resources,
please visit the companion website at
http://resources.corwin.com/CMLExcellence

Preface

Coaching All Teachers With Multilingual Learners

Coaching is a powerful professional development process that benefits all teachers, even the most experienced teachers.

—Dan Alpert (2023)

A Little Bit of History Through My Story and Why I've Wanted to Write This Book

Many, many years ago, by a twist of fate, I became an English learner (EL), but was one of the lucky ones. My parents and grandparents were educators in Juárez, México, so it was easy for me to learn a second language. I would cross the border every day to go to high school and college in El Paso. Yet, I wondered why other students struggled. About a handful of my classmates made it to the University of Texas at El Paso with me, but sadly, we didn't get to take the same courses. They were sent to remedial mathematics and English as a second language (ESL) classes. This separation from my friends stayed with me throughout the years.

I loved literature, so I decided to major in 19th-century British literature. I completed my BA with a major in English, a minor in French, and a second minor in journalism. When my former high school asked me to teach ESL, I jumped at the opportunity.

My First Encounter With Peer Coaching

After the first two weeks of teaching ESL, I realized that the curriculum was older than me and the students were quietly suffering through it. Because they saw me as someone who was only a couple of years older and more of an equal than a distant adult, we were able to team up as peer coaches and started inventing teaching/learning strategies. I thought we had invented cooperative learning because my students loved to work together to learn and solve their language problems. Later I found out that Robert Slavin had been writing about the benefits of cooperative learning and had invented key instructional strategies (Slavin, 1975). After a few mistakes I now regret, we kept working at it. I learned to listen to my students; they learned to listen to each other and coach each other, and at the end of the year when we saw their growth, we knew we had all benefited from those peer interactions.

Coaching, Mentoring, and Role Models

During a span of five decades, coaches and mentors propelled my work. I enrolled in college full time so I could keep my student visa and work as an ESL teacher. Therefore, pursuing a master's in linguistics seemed perfect. I fell in love with linguistics! Dr. Lurline Coltharp was a brilliant professor. She taught contrastive linguistics, applied linguistics, phonology, phonemics, analyzing the language of the Tirilones (popular gang jargon), and onomastics. I took them all. She became my mentor and role model. I admired her elegance, sophisticated hairstyle, taste in clothes, and flawless instructional delivery. All these courses enriched my teaching, and she took me to my first TESOL International Association (then Teachers of English to Speakers of Other Languages) conference! After that, I started presenting at conferences. I had something to offer, thanks to my students. I obtained my master's degree and my residence visa the same day.

By a twist of fate and a few detours, those conference presentations took me to the San Diego State University (SDSU) Multicultural Resource Center as a professional development coordinator assigned to work with teachers in San Bernardino, Riverside, and Indio Counties. That's where I started putting together a framework for multilingual learners (MLs were called language-minority students or English language learners in those days). I invited the greatest minds of that time (Jim Cummins, Russell Stauffer, Steve Krashen, Jana Echevarria, Luis Moll, Esteban Díaz, Barbara Flores, Bruce Joyce, Beverly Showers, and others mentioned in some of these chapters) to present and work with us. With a fellowship for a joint doctoral program between SDSU and Claremont Graduate University, I sought to learn more about staff development (an appropriate term in those days), but that was not available. Consequently, in addition to the coursework from the two universities, I decided to audit organizational development courses at the school of business at Claremont.

Collective Creativity: A Community of Learners

Those organizational development courses made a lot of sense to me. I designed a professional development institute and began to offer it out of SDSU in the Riverside, San Bernardino, Palm Springs, and Indio County Offices of Education. I called it the Multidistrict Trainer of Trainers

Institute (MTTI). MTTIs were soon replicated throughout California's county offices of education. I wanted a practical mechanism to spread knowledge as quickly as possible. Many EL teachers and coordinators who attended the MTTIs advanced in their positions and were able to spread the word in the next few years across the state and even the country (Calderón & Marsh, 1989; Calderón & Spiegel-Coleman, 1985).

The staff members of the California State Department of Education in Sacramento were putting together *Schooling and Language Minority Students: A Theoretical Framework* (1981) and participated in the MTTIs to have access to the guest researchers. During the one-week institutes, the researchers presented in the morning while my colleagues and I worked with the MTTI participants in the afternoon to convert theory into practice. The concept of cognitive academic language proficiency (CALP) was fine-tuned as Jim Cummins and Roger Shy (personal communication, October 1980) connected at the institutes. Other researchers presented on language development to enhance ESL instruction. Additionally, sheltered instruction intended to make any subject comprehensible more easily began to emerge. Pieces of a framework began to surface in my mind.

What Was Missing? Integrating More Literacy Into Language Development and More Language Development Into Literacy

After the first year, I felt that we needed more rigor, particularly when it came to teaching reading and writing. I invited several reading and writing proponents to present their knowledge and praxis, but their strategies seemed quite limited. How did I learn to read? I only remember my mom reading to me from *Las mil y una noches* (*One Thousand and One Nights*, or the *Tales of Arabian Nights*) every night. I was a reader in Spanish when I went to kindergarten. I wish I could recall transferring my Spanish reading skills into English reading. Was learning to read in Spanish a major factor in my insouciant transfer to English?

But I digress. I still wanted to reach all core content teachers in a school and create more challenging but meaningful literacy, language, and content learning for MLs in their classrooms. That's when I turned my interest to Bruce Joyce and Marsha Weil's (1980) models of teaching (*Inquiry, Concept Attainment, Concept Development, Direct Instruction, Group Investigation, Synectics, Problem Solving, Role Playing, Simulation*, and *Games*). The perfect CALP! Dr. Joyce and Dr. Beverly Showers came to the MTTIs to present those models. They would present in the morning, and in the afternoon we would add the second-language strategies that the teachers had volunteered to test in their classrooms the following week.

From Drs. Joyce and Showers, I also learned about the *concept of transfer*, key to the quality implementation of a comprehensive professional development approach that includes coaching. So, I focused on a coaching study for my dissertation by enacting the transfer trail from the MTTI into the teachers' repertoire and subsequently into the MLs' academic achievement. I randomly divided twenty-four teachers who attended the one-week MTTI into two groups—one group had coaching while another (control) group did not. Dr. Joyce became my coach, mentor, and ex officio dissertation committee member. The implementation study had great outcomes. By the end of the year, the teachers in the experimental group implemented with frequency and "creative fidelity," and their students outperformed the control students by large margins. The results are in my doctoral dissertation, *Training Bilingual Trainers: A Quantitative and Ethnographic Study of Coaching and Its Impact on the Transfer of Training* (Calderón, 1984).

From a Process to a Content Delivery Model to More Coaches and Mentors

I had the structure and process for training and coaching, with content that was still missing pieces. As I visited a variety of classrooms beyond the purview of the study, I saw that MLs were not reading enough. Teachers read to them, or they would be off in a corner pretending to read.

What's more, by another fantastic twist of fate, one day while I was observing ESL teachers in a school, I saw a presenter from Johns Hopkins University (JHU) training elementary teachers (but not ESL teachers) with Cooperative Integrated Reading and Composition (CIRC), and I loved it! I wrote to Dr. Slavin at JHU, and we decided to meet at the American Educational Research Association (AERA) conference that month. He would tell me all about CIRC, and I would tell him all about my dissertation on professional development and coaching, and how we were quickly reaching broad audiences beyond California. He was getting ready to scale up Success for All (SFA). Dr. Slavin is a renowned researcher who empirically studied reading and cooperative learning and developed the SFA program to teach reading foundations (phonemic awareness, phonics, vocabulary, fluency, and comprehension) from prekindergarten to the sixth grade (Slavin & Madden, 2001). This program is still widely used. When I met Dr. Slavin, he expressed interest in learning more about MLs and asked if I would contribute to his proposal for an Institute of Education Sciences (IES) grant.

That semester, I finished my dissertation and went to teach at the University of California at Santa Barbara. I taught at UCSB for four years, but I couldn't do the type of research I wanted because there were hardly any MLs in the schools at that time. I was already receiving funds from JHU because Dr. Slavin's Center for Research on the Education of

Students Placed at Risk (CRESPAR) had been funded by IES. As much as I hated to leave lovely Santa Barbara, I decided to go to El Paso, Texas, where I knew there were many MLs, and I could conduct a formal study.

In Ysleta Independent School District, I was able to conduct a comprehensive five-year study on reading for MLs in five experimental and control schools. Dr. Slavin became my coach and mentor along with Rachel Hertz-Lazarowitz from Haifa University. We published "Effects of Bilingual Cooperative Integrated Reading and Composition on Students Making the Transition From Spanish to English Reading" (Calderón et al., 1998). Since 1998, Bilingual Cooperative Integrated Reading and Composition (BCIRC) is the only comprehensive bilingual reading study in the What Works Clearinghouse. This study helped me to see how students can use both languages for learning.

Somewhere along that lovely part of the journey, I took some parallel twists to participate in a joint JHU/Harvard/Center for Applied Linguistics (CAL)/Miami University research project on the transfer from reading in Spanish to reading in English. The study took place in experimental and control schools in El Paso, Chicago, and Massachusetts. It was most insightful working with Catherine Snow, Diane August, Maria Carlo, and some young researchers. The seven-year study was funded by the National Institute of Child Health and Human Development (August et al., 2001).

When I served on the National Literacy Panel on Language-Minority Children and Youth (August & Shanahan, 2006), I learned more about reading for MLs in the early grades and the cross-linguistic features that enhance or delay learning a second language. I contributed to professional learning and coaching when I co-authored Chapter 8, "Instruction and Professional Development" (August et al., 2008), in the panel's follow-up practitioner's book *Developing Reading and Writing in Second-Language Learners: Lessons From the Report of the National Literacy Panel on Language-Minority Children and Youth* (August & Shanahan, 2008).

While in El Paso, I was invited to join the faculty at the University of Texas at El Paso's Department of Educational Leadership. During those class interactions, I learned about the perils and successes principals experience as they attempt to implement a whole-school approach for ML success. I also worked with El Paso Independent School District on a study (Calderón & Carreón, 2001) funded by JHU and published by Corwin, *Designing and Implementing Two-Way Bilingual Programs* (Calderón & Minaya-Rowe, 2003). Oh, and I became a U.S. citizen then.

Mentored for Research on Reading for MLs

I look back to the reading models that Dr. Slavin started in the 1990s and were included in the National Reading Panel (2000) report. His K–5 programs had all the features and the sequence that most publishers and state departments of education are currently attempting to implement as the Science of Reading. Way ahead of the reading debates and perplexity, Dr. Slavin soon developed two versions of SFA that were designed for MLs—*SFA ESL Reading* and the *Éxito Para Todos* version in Spanish.

At the end of the fourth year of my BCIRC study, we decided it was time for me to be part of the JHU faculty of education. The Carnegie Corporation of New York had asked me to develop and test a BCIRC-type model for middle and high schools—grade levels that had been my first love and experience! With the new title of professor/senior research scientist at JHU, I set about designing another longitudinal study to test in four New York City and Kauai experimental and control schools. Students in the experimental schools outperformed those in the control schools again. That study became Expediting Comprehension for English Language Learners (ExC-ELL) (Calderón, 2007; see also exc-ell.com/publications).

When I began to replicate both BCIRC and ExC-ELL, I learned new nomenclature for the skills that students develop through cooperative learning. These are currently called social-emotional competencies. Other ideas soon emerged in schools such as translanguaging, multiliteracies, multimodalities, and building on students' assets. Hence, I continue to learn new terminology; to build on the evidence-based features of language and literacy instruction; and, as we coach teachers across the country, to learn more about coaching for transfer from teacher delivery to the students' academic learning. Since 1984, transfer from training remains the pillar of quality implementation, as evidenced by visible and quantifiable improved student gains when compared to non-transfer-enactments schools.

Empirical Testing of the Whole-School Learning and Coaching Model

Recently, with a U.S. Department of Education National Professional Development grant, the ExC-ELL model was studied as a whole-school professional learning and coaching approach in Virginia's middle and high schools. Although intended to be a descriptive study, the systems approach to implementation was quantifiably substantiated by data from my coaching observations, district coaches' protocols and reports, student scores, and interviews (Calderón & Tartaglia, 2023; Zacarian et al., 2021). With this study, the ExC-ELL whole-school approach was tested and refined further. ExC-ELL continues to be implemented in hundreds of schools in the United States and abroad. The chapters to come describe its academic language, reading comprehension, writing components, supportive instructional strategies, and techniques (social-emotional learning, cooperative learning, metacognition, and student tools) for coaching each component.

The Evolution of This Professional Learning and Coaching Model

This has been a long journey. There have been many victories, mistakes, disappointments, heartbreaks, and great insights and successes derived from these milestones:

1980—Collaboration by Bruce Joyce and Beverly Showers with our teachers

1984—The study of coaching in experimental and control bilingual classrooms

1998—BCIRC study of (1) transfer from Spanish into English, (2) the professional development model, (3) teacher learning communities (TLCs), and (4) coaching bilingual and ESL teachers

2001—Collaborative randomized study of transfer of reading skills from Spanish to English, by JHU, Harvard, CAL, and Miami University

2007—Empirical study of ExC-ELL vocabulary, reading, and writing integrated into core content subjects in New York and Kauai experimental and control secondary schools; refinement of coaching, TLCs, and how low-performing schools moved quickly to exemplary status

2017—Ethnographic study of the whole-school approach to the ExC-ELL components, professional development, coaching, and TLC approaches in middle and high schools

2019—A rapid switch and adaptation to online teacher professional development and coaching for supporting thousands of educators

2023—A hybrid adaptation (in-person and online) for teacher development, TLCs, and coaching

Most "innovations" in the field of teaching and learning build on existing trajectories of research and practice. As one might surmise from this outline, my approach to both coaching and instruction has been built on a distinguished legacy of empirical research as well as practical application. I reference seminal research studies because these older studies were and still are the foundation of more current research and practice. For instance, what we now call the Science of Reading stems from studies published in the year 2000 (National Reading Panel, 2000) and for English learners in 2006 and 2008 (August et al., 2008; August & Shanahan, 2006, 2008). Most contemporary studies on coaching cite Joyce and Showers's (1982, 2002) pioneering studies or those who cited them. Now, many contemporary researchers of literacy and/or coaching continue to build on these rocks.

One of my goals has been to bridge coaching and effective instruction for MLs. My research has shown great outcomes in the past and continues to evolve to meet the contemporary needs of MLs, their teachers, and their schools.

Despite all the evidence-based studies, my concept of a whole-school approach to preparing everyone at the school and improving systems for MLs often falls on rocky ground or thorns. Maybe I push too hard or not hard enough. The concept of comprehensive professional development for the whole school that includes coaching is accepted only by the best and the brightest. The goodwill of others is often squashed by a shortage of funds or a fear of leaving the status quo. Still, decades of studies and encounters with schools have contributed to the continued refinement of this professional learning framework. We see the tremendous results when schools recognize and enact the concept of transfer and the impact it can have on MLs and all other students in the school. In this book, I try to highlight features that can be replicated in your school and steps for quality implementation of this or any professional learning and coaching design.

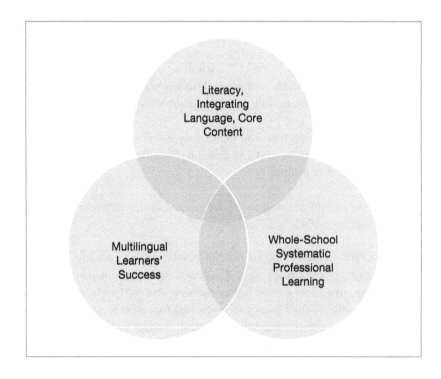

Acknowledgments

All My Coaches

I am so grateful to Dan Alpert for being such an amazing champion of equity for multilingual multicultural students and their educators! Dan's ideas have greatly enriched the writing of the Corwin multilingual, dual-language, equity team. He has made our writing a delightful and pleasant endeavor. So many of my colleagues and I will miss him so much! He was my first editor for my first Corwin book and launched me into the love of writing.

Now, I am grateful to Megan Bedell, Mia Rodriguez, Tori Mirsadjadi, and Melinda Masson, who inherited this book and immediately took it to heart. With their expertise, we didn't have to skip a beat.

I asked the following amazing team of trainers, facilitators, and coaches who work with me to contribute their recommendations for other coaches: Lisa Tartaglia, Hector Montenegro, Leticia Trower, Karen Solis, Lillian Ardell, Cristina Zakis, Giulianna J. Lewis, Alyson Reilly, and Rebecca Upchurch. After so many years of coaching and training educators with me, I wanted to highlight their expertise and the contributions they have made to our professional development process and products. Leticia also contributed the art summaries and the virtual version tools for coaching online. Nanci Esparza provided artwork as well, and her assistance with the references was invaluable.

I also asked several of my colleagues, the ones I call rock stars, to contribute their insights on coaching for the readers: Margo Gottlieb, Andrea Honigsfeld, Mariana Castro, Karen Brock, Debbie Zacarian, and Rubi Flores. I am most grateful for their words of wisdom that bring up critical issues we need to keep in mind.

Of course, we all need friends-as-readers: Rebecca Fitch, Amy Anderson, Kris McLaughlin, and Luis Palomares provided wonderful feedback. Luis was kind enough to go through the text meticulously and edit out many of the blunders we English-as-a-second-language learners still carry around.

Publisher's Acknowledgments

Corwin gratefully acknowledges the contributions of the following reviewers:

Altagracia H. Delgado
Executive Director of Multilingual Services
Aldine ISD
Houston, TX

Michelle Strom
Grade 5–8 Teacher
DoDEA, Europe South
Vicenza, Italy

About the Author

Dr. Margarita Espino Calderón, born and raised in Juárez, México, is a professor emerita/senior research scientist at Johns Hopkins University. Her research and development projects have been funded by the U.S. Department of Education, the National Institutes of Health, the U.S. Department of Labor, the Carnegie Corporation of New York, and various state offices of education. One of her empirical studies, Bilingual Cooperative Integrated Reading and Composition (BCIRC), is featured in the What Works Clearinghouse. The Carnegie Corporation of New York funded her five-year study to develop Expediting Comprehension for English Language Learners (ExC-ELL) to train mathematics, science, social studies, language arts, and English as a second language (ESL) teachers on integrating language, reading, and content in core content middle and high school classrooms. With a Title III National Professional Development grant, she implemented a whole-school approach to professional development with ExC-ELL in Loudoun County, Virginia. She replicated this approach in twenty-nine schools in Texas and North Carolina. She served on the National Literacy Panel on Language-Minority Children and Youth, the Carnegie Corporation of New York English Language Adolescent Literacy Panel, and other panels and national committees. She has over one hundred publications on language, literacy, and professional development. Her latest Corwin publications include the following:

Calderón, M. E., & Slakk, S. (2020). From language to language, literacy, and content. In M. E. Calderón, M. Dove, D. S. Fenner, M. Gottlieb, A. Honigsfeld, T. W. Singer, S. Slakk, I. Soto, & D. Zacarian (Ed.), *Breaking down the wall: Essential shifts for English learners' success* (pp. 111–134). Corwin.

Soto, I., Snyder, S., Calderón, E. M., Gottlieb, M., Honigsfeld, A., Lachance, J., Marshal, M., Nungaray, D., Flores, R., & Scott, L. (2023). *Breaking down the monolingual wall: Essential shifts for multilingual learners' success.* Corwin.

Zacarian, D., Calderón, M. E., & Gottlieb, M. (2021). *Beyond crises: Overcoming linguistic and cultural inequities in communities, schools and classrooms.* Corwin.

Introduction

. . . .

Coaching Teachers
With Multilingual Learners
in Their Classrooms

 EXTRA, EXTRA, READ ALL ABOUT IT!

ExC-ELL DAILY NEWS

- Approximately 5.3 million English learners are in our schools.
- Schools may have between 25% and 75% long-term English learners.
- Nearly a million new migrants came to the United States in 2021–2022, many of whom are children.
- There is a critical English-as-a-second-language and bilingual teacher shortage.

Graphic created with Canva by Leticia M. Trower.

Sources: Batalova (2024), National Center for Education Statistics (2024), Regional Educational Laboratory West (2016), and Williams (2023).

*T*hese days, coaches must have the background knowledge and skills to address the diverse linguistic, cultural, academic, and social-emotional needs of multilingual learners who are now in practically every school in the United States. This book is written specifically for coaches who have the exciting opportunity of coaching teachers in schools that already are serving or will soon serve the needs of multilingual learners.

> The abbreviation *MLs* will be used to represent all the categories or terms applied across the country to English learners and/or multilingual learners. Chapter 2 presents the diversity in detail.

As MLs continue to arrive, all teachers in every school will need coaches who have second-language instructional strategies and philosophies among their extensive knowledge base. Coaches who have this base will be highly sought after. For instance, the newly arrived multilingual students in elementary schools must have support from a language specialist (English as a second language [ESL] or English language development [ELD] teacher) as required by state and federal legislature. The ESL/ELD teacher helps the general education teacher usually during language arts by working with the newcomer for a specified time. However, due to ESL and bilingual teacher shortages, the ESL/ELD specialist will most likely need to assist four or more teachers in the school and will not be able to stay long in one classroom. This means that the general education teachers will be left on their own for the rest of the day after the ESL/ELD teacher leaves. This is when the coach will be most welcome!

In secondary schools, core content teachers are too many and the subjects too diverse for there to be adequate language assistance from specialists in every classroom all day long as recommended by the U.S. Department of Justice Civil Rights Division and U.S. Department of Education Office for Civil Rights (2015) and the U.S. Department of Education Office of English Language Acquisition (2023). Therefore, middle and high school teachers will benefit greatly from a coach who is learning or has learned about second-language acquisition for integrating principles and practices into all subjects.

> Core content teachers do not want to water down their expectations. They want to know how to reach MLs with the appropriate evidence-based scaffolds.

All teachers benefit from coaching that specializes in second-language acquisition, including knowing how to integrate academic language, reading comprehension, and writing skills into the content area being taught. Additionally, given the setback from the COVID-19 pandemic that stifled language development and affected national reading and social studies scores (mathematics could also stand improvement) for all students, every teacher wants to know what to do to help students.

When teachers and coaches receive quality preparation to enhance instructional practices that can integrate subject knowledge with academic language, reading, and writing skills, all students will benefit, not just MLs. In the following chapters, I will discuss how to better respond to the social-emotional needs of students, particularly new arrivals to the country, and how culturally responsive knowledge by their teachers also plays a big role in coaching.

> The way we've done teaching and coaching since 2020 does not meet our current needs.

Coaches continue to ask us for new observational protocols and a better process of support. They feel that existing observation protocols and checklists for coaches of teachers with MLs need considerable adaptation. Coaches and teachers can systematically strengthen their knowledge of theories and evidence-based research that undergirds the development of MLs' language, literacy, and content areas with new research and practices. These new practices can also help develop cultural understanding and sensitivity to the assets students bring. This view of students will fortify a coach's feedback during student engagement, the detailed perceptions of teacher and student talk, and the use of social-emotional competencies by both teachers and students.

How We Can Adapt Coaching

In the past ten years, there have been many books and articles on coaching (Aguilar, 2013; Bright Morning, 2024; Costa & Garmston, 2015; Hattie, 2009, 2012; Knight, 2019, 2021) and randomized studies (Garet et al., 2001; Hill et al., 2018; Kelcey et al., 2019; Kraft & Hill, 2020) that affirm the value of coaching. We can all learn from the valuable ideas in these resources that apply to multilingual multiliteracy coaching.

> The term *multilingual/multiliteracy coaches* (*ML coaches*) is used to represent the coaches who support teachers teaching MLs.

For example, Edwards's (2024) synthesis of school-based studies on Cognitive Coaching (Costa & Garmston, 2015) lists studies that describe teacher satisfaction and benefits to teachers, how Cognitive Coaching built strength and ability in teachers and principals, and how teachers changed their views and practices about teaching students. Some studies mention multilingual students, and a handful of studies mention evidence-based student growth (Edwards, 2024).

The value of Cognitive Coaching for multilingual coaches is the goal of producing self-directed persons to be self-managing, self-monitoring, and self-modifying (Edwards, 2024). This goal applies to the efforts coaches will be making as they manage, monitor, and modify their current practices to fit the new student populations and new requests for help from a different type of teacher whom they are unaccustomed to supporting.

There is one issue to consider from all these studies: Empirical experimental and control studies on coaching that measure effects on MLs specifically are yet to emerge and be disseminated. Just as with the National Reading Panel (2000) report, the authors only mention that MLs were part of the studies, but the data were not desegregated.

We can assume that Cognitive Coaching and other coaching programs have been effective with MLs, but why are so many long-term MLs, those who have been in our schools for many years, still underachieving? Why does it take so long for newcomers to learn English? Why aren't more schools adopting the type of coaching that yields outstanding outcomes for MLs?

Fortunately, there are some studies and theories of practice that we can apply or adapt to prepare ML coaches—particularly those who focus squarely on instructional practice. Knight (2021) tells us how coaches can partner with teachers to (1) establish a clear picture of reality; (2) set emotionally compelling, student-focused goals; and (3) learn, adapt, and integrate teaching practices that help teachers and students hit goals (Knight, 2022, Preface). Knight's ideas relate to coaching teachers with MLs because educators need a clearer picture of (1) what quality instruction looks like in multilingual classrooms; (2) how to focus on MLs' strengths and assets instead of deficits, removing past biases and misconceptions as the first step to setting appropriate goals; and (3) how all core content teachers need to learn, adapt, and integrate into their core content lessons language, social-emotional competencies, and literacy practices.

Knight's (2022) seven success factors for instructional coaching (partnership, communication, leadership, coaching process, data, instructional playbook, and system support) that must be in place for coaches to flourish apply to ML coaches. Discussion on these factors will be woven into the instructional chapters and the final chapter.

The Prevalent Process of Coaching

Coaching in multilingual/multicultural classrooms can take the form of the *prevalent or familiar coaching* cycle, demonstrated in Figure I.1: planning the observation and data collection, conducting the observation, teacher and coach analyzing the data from the observation, teacher and coach reflecting on the results of the analysis, and planning the next steps. The communication techniques, the process, and the responsibilities of the participant are basically the same in most coaching approaches used today. *It is the content or focus of the observation and feedback that changes.*

Figure I.1   The Familiar Coaching Process

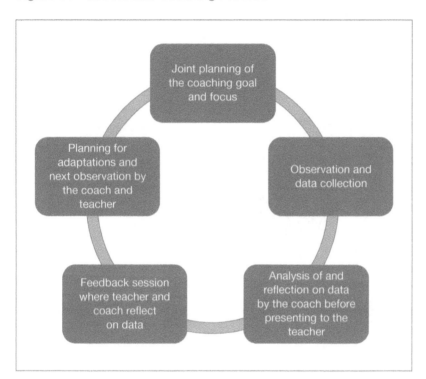

The Proposed Focus of Coaching in Multilingual Classrooms

Impact on learning and excelling in academic language and literacy is the content target for coaching in classrooms with MLs. As shown in Figure I.2, teachers of MLs simultaneously address language, literacy, and content development. Instruction stems from an assets-based mindset about MLs. Observations, data collection, and feedback are specific to improving language, as well as literacy integrated into content development and outcomes. This specificity is what has been missing from most existing types of coaching.

Figure I.2   Content for Coaching in Today's Schools

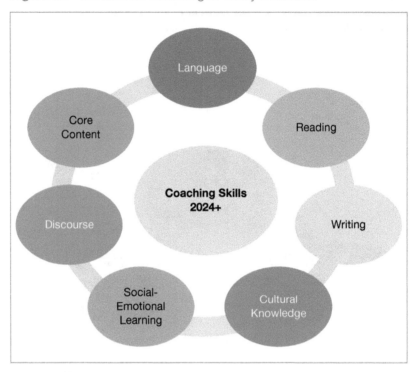

Source: Graphic by Leticia M. Trower

online resources   Available for download at http://resources.corwin.com/CMLExcellence

The Purpose of This Book

The purpose of this book is to provide a language, literacy, and content framework with the comprehensive instructional strategies that teachers of MLs can implement to help MLs succeed, and the strategies and coaching protocols that coaches can use to actuate teachers' quality implementation. This comprehensive example of a framework is not one-size-fits-all. For instruction to be effective for MLs, a whole-school framework must put these students at the center. Ways of ensuring a quality implementation supported by coaches are the focus.

We want to highlight the areas where coaches can adjust their preparation to effectively work with general education teachers. Due to the high demand to provide effective coaching for middle and high schools, many of the suggestions and examples here are dedicated to Grade 6–12 teachers of mathematics, science, social studies, language arts, and all other subjects who have one, a handful, or a classroom full of MLs. Teachers will realize that the instructional strategies described here apply to every subject because students need to discuss, read, and write in every subject. Moreover, most state tests now require reading and written explanations that are dependent on a rich vocabulary repertoire.

Coaches who work with ESL/ELD teachers within self-contained classrooms or who team-teach with K–12 teachers will also find this extremely useful, including for coaching dual-language teachers or sheltered instruction teachers at K–12 schools.

Processes and strategies were tested in different coaching situations, conditions, and contexts: expert external ML coaches, site-based coaches, peer/collegial coaches, co-teachers as coaches, students as peer coaches, and administrators/supervisors as coaches. Administrators go through the same professional learning sessions to provide support for teachers.

In the upcoming chapters you will see all of the following:

▶ Instructional strategies focused on the language domains: listening, speaking, reading, writing, and thinking

▶ Teacher and coach discourse woven into vignettes

▶ Social-emotional strategies that can be easily taught during each domain

▶ Ways to prepare students to work in pairs or teams to accelerate language interaction, increase depth of reading comprehension, and improve writing

▶ Contributions by nationally known coaches and experienced multilingual/multicultural coaches working in or with multilingual/multicultural schools that include their views, experiences, successes, challenges, and resiliency tips

▶ In-chapter instructional strategies followed by suggestions for "what coaches do"

▶ Reflection questions with space for notes, offered for collegial discussions, problem solutions, and contemplating next steps

▶ End-of-chapter graphic summaries highlighting the main points and/or practical checklists

▶ End-of-chapter comments from teachers, coaches, and principals for you and your colleagues to discuss and begin to build a road map toward student, teacher, coach, and whole-school success

Chapter 1: Coaching—What It Is and What It Is Yet to Be

Elaborating on "why" it is time to enhance coaching practices in all the schools, Chapter 1 describes and builds upon extensive prior and current research on the benefits of coaching as described in the Preface. It lays out the process for transfer from the workshop/learning event into a teacher's instructional repertoire, the administrator's implementation responsibility, and a student's learning accountability. Perhaps *the most important why of coaching is the transfer and impact on MLs' learning.* Connections to MLs' academic success in middle and high school are made.

> Transfer is typically overlooked in most professional development initiatives.

Chapter 2: What Do Instructional Coaches Need to Know to Coach Teachers With Multilingual Learners?

Chapter 2 describes the diversity of MLs and their needs. According to the U.S. Department of Education, there were approximately 5.3 million English learners (ELs) in American public schools in the fall of 2021 (National Center for Education Statistics, 2024). *English learner* is still the official term used by the Departments of Education and Justice, although the terms *multilingual learner* and *emergent bilingual* are now preferred by educators. Not surprisingly, there are other terms to consider as well. Some categories, moreover, are not included in the formal count.

The ever-growing number of MLs is compounded by students who have not yet been identified as MLs. Requirements from the U.S. Department of Justice Civil Rights Division and U.S. Department of Education Office for Civil Rights (2023) call for state education agencies to monitor local schools and districts to make sure the following occurs:

- MLs are promptly and properly identified.

- MLs have meaningful access to grade-level content.

- All ML teachers are well prepared.

- Programs include English proficiency benchmarks to ensure that MLs are making progress in learning English and that steps are taken if they are not.

- MLs who exit the EL category and no longer need ESL support must be monitored for two years after demonstrating the capacity to do ordinary work in English, and remedies must be provided when needed.

> In addition to the compliance requirements, there is a moral commitment to help all students excel in school.

Chapter 3: Coaching Reading Teaching and Learning

Reading is a student's most valuable tool. Students in middle and high school need good reading skills to succeed in mathematics, science, social studies, language arts, and other classes. Vocabulary/academic language is a subcomponent of reading comprehension that undergirds information processing, critical thinking, and rich discussions about what students read. We know that MLs are not reading enough. They can accelerate their reading skills with specific strategies that were developed for and tested with MLs. In Chapter 3, we address these questions:

▶ What does the research say about reading for MLs?

▶ Why do these reading strategies work for all students?

▶ What reading strategies work in all subject areas?

▶ How do we coach teaching reading? Are there sentence stems or discussion starters for coaches to use?

▶ How do we observe MLs and collect what type of data to know if they are becoming proficient readers?

▶ How do we collect data for coaching on student interaction during reading activities?

▶ What social-emotional discourse can we look for during reading practice?

▶ What observation protocols, processes, and tools in English and other languages can teachers and coaches use?

Chapter 4: Coaching Vocabulary and Discourse

Vocabulary is a huge part of literacy. Because it is a subcomponent of reading, it behooves teachers and coaches to be well versed in the features of language and the most effective and efficient instructional strategies for teaching vocabulary. Teachers introduce key vocabulary from the text or projects that students are about to encounter in class to help them comprehend and master the content.

We have been hit hard by surprising results from the national mathematics, social studies, and reading outcomes. Yet, we are also dealing with years of injustice because the achievement gaps between whites, Latinos, and Blacks existed long before COVID-19. Changes that need to be made are difficult. Perhaps this is the time to coalesce changes that have evidence of being effective with MLs and other striving readers that can be implemented easily with the professional development process described in Chapters 1 and 6.

MLs have always been left behind due to not enough language instruction being connected to content texts or reading strategies for the diverse expository texts used in secondary schools. Sharing the research, premises, and tested strategies used with MLs in longitudinal studies, this chapter is organized around some questions we are typically asked:

▶ Why is preteaching vocabulary before every lesson critically important for MLs?

▶ How do we help teachers recognize the language demands of standards-based lessons and units?

▶ How can we be more deliberate, explicit, and methodical about teaching vocabulary, academic language, and academic discourse?

▶ Which words should we select to preteach?

▶ How do we teach a word/phrase?

▶ How do we coach vocabulary teaching strategies? Are there sentence stems or talking points for coaching this?

▶ How do we observe MLs and know if they are learning vocabulary?

▶ How do we coach student conversations?

▶ What is the role of native language instruction and translanguaging?

▶ What social-emotional discourse can we look for during vocabulary practice?

▶ What observation protocols, processes, and tools can be used by English and bilingual/dual-language teachers and coaches?

Chapter 5: Coaching Writing

Language is the basis of powerful writing. Once students have learned vocabulary from a mentor text and practiced using it before reading, during reading, and after reading, they can feel confident and properly tooled to do content-based writing. Chapter 5 addresses the following questions:

▶ What does the research tell us about writing for MLs?

▶ What writing strategies tap cultural appreciation as well as creativity, originality, and talents?

▶ How do we observe writing?

▶ How do we coach peer interactions during writing?

▶ What social-emotional discourse can we look for during vocabulary practice?

▶ How do we coach writing instruction and give feedback on assessing student writing? Are there sentence stems or discussion points for coaching?

▶ What observation protocols, processes, and tools can be used by English and bilingual/dual-language teachers and coaches?

Chapter 6: Creating a Whole-School Approach to Coaching

It takes a whole-school effort to plan and ensure the implementation of teachers' and coaches' new knowledge, skills, and dispositions. No school can afford to think that one ESL teacher and one coach will make a difference by themselves.

Topics in Chapter 6 concentrate on the transfer of learning into the classroom and the impact it can have on MLs and all other students:

▶ Professional development for teachers and coaches—together

▶ Types of teams for peer coaching

▶ Bracing for resistance and ways to deal with it

▶ In-person and virtual coaching options—and the benefits of each

▶ What works and what is doable

▶ Acknowledging precious time and ways of scheduling

▶ Assessing and addressing to what extent coaches and teachers are involved in this endeavor

▶ Data to gauge transfer from training and quality of implementation

▶ A summary of linguistically and culturally proficient coaching

Linguistically and culturally responsive coaching entails frequent analysis of implementation. To what extent are teachers implementing this model? How effective is the relationship between teacher and coach? Research shows that program implementation supported by comprehensive professional development is much more successful than buying a packaged program (Calderón, 2007; Short & Fitzsimmons, 2007). This book provides a content and process framework for coaches and teachers to learn in situ. It begins with a joint professional development program, followed by the application of their new knowledge in the classroom. Mistakes will be necessary to move forward together. Without taking risks and knowing mistakes are useful, we sustain the status quo.

More than ever, there's a great urgency to examine critically our attitudes, skills, and practices when working with MLs to improve teaching and learning. The goal of this book is to help coaches and teachers make that shift—perhaps you have been wanting to make these changes but need a little nudge and a couple of practical tools to help you and your colleagues look at diversity in new ways and enact what you already know can close those gaps. I celebrate the coaches who continue to make a powerful impact on multilingual students and classroom peers.

Coaching— What It Is and What It Is Yet to Be

CHAPTER #1

From One Coach to Another: Tips for Coaches of Teachers With Multilingual Learners

It's important to meet teachers where they are, being mindful not to overwhelm them with too many things at once. Start with one new strategy or idea, then make sure the teacher understands it fully, including how it can benefit students and what it might look like in their classroom context (considering the student population, content area, lesson topic, classroom structure, etc.). If your role allows, offer to support the teacher with their implementation as needed, whether that's modeling the strategy, co-delivering the lesson, or observing the teacher while they try it out. Then, be sure to debrief how it goes, using the debrief as an opportunity to highlight and celebrate successes as well as make any suggestions regarding possible adjustments or address any questions. Finally, identify concrete next steps that support the teacher in further supporting their students. Even for the best teachers, implementing new strategies and approaches can feel overwhelming. The best thing you can do as a coach is to help teachers (and their students!) have a low-risk, high-reward experience.

—Rebecca Upchurch, Instructional Coach, Loudoun County Public Schools; CEO and Clarity and Mindset Coach, Higher Good Coaching

Many schools and districts have been employing or describing coaching practices for many years (Aguilar, 2013; Bright Morning, 2024; Calderón, 1984, 2007; Calderón & Tartaglia, 2023; Costa & Garmston, 2015; Edwards, 2024; Fullan, 2001; Instructional Coaching Group, n.d.; Joyce & Showers, 1982a, 1982b; Killion et al., 2020; Knight, 2007, 2019, 2022; Lieberman, 1995). Although coaching takes many forms and interpretations, it is typically characterized by a one-on-one relationship between a coach and a teacher. The relationship focuses on supporting a teacher's instructional improvement. Coaches typically support teachers by modeling *classroom practices, observing teachers' instruction, facilitating critical self-reflection, providing direct feedback,* and *facilitating school-based learning communities.* Teachers and coaches work together in this reciprocal relationship to improve teacher efficacy and student learning while focusing on equity (Aguilar, 2020; Darling-Hammond & McLaughlin, 1995; Joyce & Showers, 2002; Knight, 2007).

Coaching can be a powerful tool to help teachers who are new to teaching multicultural students with diverse language and literacy levels. While research is scarce on how coaching helps secondary-level core content teachers integrate language and literacy into their teaching repertoire, there is enough proof that coaching can work effectively (Calderón, 2007; Calderón & Tartaglia, 2023; Zacarian et al., 2021).

Theoretical and Research Basis for Coaching Teachers With Multilingual Learners

Findings for multilingual learners (MLs) and multicultural classrooms and programs from the National Literacy Panel on Language-Minority Children and Youth (August & Shanahan, 2006, 2008) are summarized here:

- Well-trained coaches and teachers make a difference in teacher and student outcomes.

- Regardless of the program (structured English immersion, transitional bilingual, dual-language, two-way bilingual, or general classroom), what matters most is teacher quality and the quality of the professional development programs.

- There are features unique to the professional development of teachers who work with MLs.

- Creating change in teachers is a time-consuming process and involves an outside collaborator.

- Professional development on MLs must be continuous for several years.

- Practices and beliefs change with training and application in the classroom.

Research has suggested that the transfer of ideas from traditional professional development into actual instructional change and an increase in student learning is extremely limited (e.g., Garet et al., 2001). Most professional development in multilingual settings has been the proverbial one-shot workshop on theories about second-language acquisition or a medley of strategies usually attended by volunteer English as a second language (ESL) teachers who often already have that knowledge.

They are sent to workshops and conferences to learn and turnkey those learnings with other teachers in the schools in one-hour workshops. Coaching in those instances is very rare, and that leads to little transfer into the classroom and dismal impact on MLs.

Figure 1.1   Transfer From Workshop to Quality Implementation

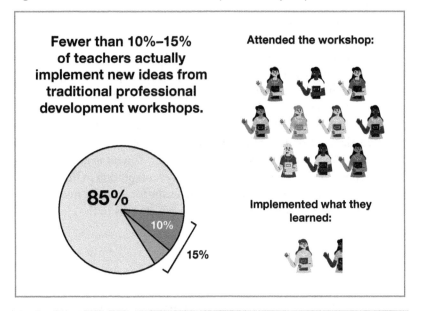

Source: Graphic by Leticia M. Trower

online resources   Available for download at http://resources.corwin.com/CMLExcellence

Joyce and Showers (1982a, 1982b, 2002) found that only 10–15 percent of teachers actually implement new ideas from traditional professional development workshops because they lack the knowledge needed for implementation and lack support and feedback to guide their implementation (see Figure 1.1). As schools respond to mounting pressures to adopt policies that improve teaching and learning, they are often tasked with connecting state- and district-level policies with teacher practice (Woulfin & Jones, 2018). For example, administrators move from one reading curriculum model to another without giving teachers enough time to embrace it and adapt it to their students. When coaching is part of the model, coaches experience the same time limitations for proper implementation.

We know that multilingual learners should be provided with opportunities to observe, discuss, and reflect with others; practice application of new ideas; and receive feedback from a more capable peer (Tharp & Gallimore, 1988). Teachers learning new skills also need modeling and practice with feedback that leads to quality implementation of new instructional practices (Instructional Coaching Group, n.d.). Research affirms that coaches can have a significant impact on teachers' skills (August & Shanahan, 2006, 2008; Garet et al., 2001; Instructional Coaching Group, n.d.; Joyce & Showers, 1982a, 1982b, 2002; Tharp & Gallimore, 1988; Woulfin & Jones, 2018). However, navigating varying school and district contexts, coaches must also navigate different policy environments. In some instances, coaches are assigned to tasks that distract from their primary role—to support and enhance teachers' quality instructional delivery and student learning.

During a series of workshops—the Multidistrict Trainer of Trainers Institutes (MTTIs) conducted in Southern California between 1981 and 1982—Bruce Joyce, Beverly Showers, and Rachel Hertz-Lazarowitz forecasted what would happen after the workshops if coaching was not implemented. Their previous studies (Hertz-Lazarowitz et al., 1980; Joyce & Showers, 2002; Showers et al., 1980) indicated that the transfer of knowledge and skill into the classroom could have a high impact (from 1.0 to 1.69 effect sizes) or barely an impact on student academic attainment, depending on the frequency, fidelity, or adaptation of implementation. When we work with a school, we can easily forecast the quality of the outcomes at the end of the year after a couple of visits to the classrooms.

Transfer From Training Into the Active Teaching Repertoire

When a professional development institute or workshop combines (1) theory, research, and basic principles, (2) modeling of instructional strategies by facilitators, and (3) practice by participants, the majority of the participants are prepared to implement the innovation. However, without coaching after the workshop, most of the teachers stop using the new strategies in a few weeks. Worse yet, there is minimal impact on the intended students.

Transfer from a teacher's professional learning

to the teacher's daily planning and teaching repertoire

to the impact on students' language, literacy, and content knowledge

On the other hand, when Hertz-Lazarowitz and colleagues (1980) trained Arab and Hebrew teachers and followed their set of workshops with systematic coaching, the results were overwhelmingly positive. Eighty-five percent of the teachers sustained the innovation to the end of the year, and the student growth was twice as large as they had expected (Hertz-Lazarowitz et al., 1980).

Replication of the Studies in California

In the 1984 study (Calderón, 1984), we began to map out the transfer from the professional development workshops to the teachers' active teaching repertoire and then to the student gains (see Figure 1.2).

Figure 1.2 Tracking Transfer

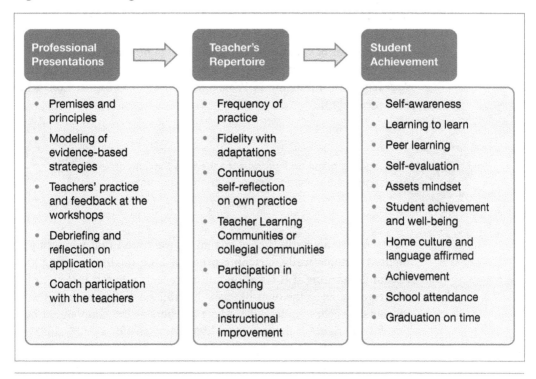

Professional Presentations

- Premises and principles
- Modeling of evidence-based strategies
- Teachers' practice and feedback at the workshops
- Debriefing and reflection on application
- Coach participation with the teachers

Teacher's Repertoire

- Frequency of practice
- Fidelity with adaptations
- Continuous self-reflection on own practice
- Teacher Learning Communities or collegial communities
- Participation in coaching
- Continuous instructional improvement

Student Achievement

- Self-awareness
- Learning to learn
- Peer learning
- Self-evaluation
- Assets mindset
- Student achievement and well-being
- Home culture and language affirmed
- Achievement
- School attendance
- Graduation on time

online resources Available for download at http://resources.corwin.com/CMLExcellence

As described in the Preface, the two-year study in bilingual/ESL classrooms in Southern California consisted of a three-week professional development institute on second-language acquisition, models of teaching, and reading with follow-up coaching for the experimental teachers (Calderón, 1984; Calderón & Marsh, 1989; Calderón & Spiegel-Coleman, 1985).

Twenty-four teachers who participated in the workshops were selected and randomly separated into two groups: Group A was coached once a month, and Group B was not coached. By the end of the year, 80 percent of Group A teachers were still implementing the strategies with frequency, fidelity to the key components, and creativity. Only 30 percent of Group B teachers were implementing the strategies. Twice as many students in Cohort A were able to transition out of limited English proficient status as compared to Cohort B.

Thus, a powerful model was designed where not only first-class content was delivered but—just as important—the follow-up coaching proved to be the most powerful instrument in ensuring impact on multilingual students' language, literacy, and content learning (Calderón, 1984; Calderón & Marsh, 1989; Calderón & Spiegel-Coleman, 1985).

Since then, other schools have used the same comprehensive professional development plus coaching model (Calderón, 2007, 2016; Calderón & Tartaglia, 2023). Unfortunately, since 1984, we continue to see the chasm between professional development activities with coaching, which have an impact on MLs' learning, and those schools without follow-up coaching. Perhaps that is one of the reasons there are such large numbers of long-term MLs across the country and an ever-growing achievement gap for minoritized students on the yearly National Assessment of Educational Progress (National Center for Education Statistics, 2023).

 Coaches guide and support teachers as they integrate rigorous language and literacy into core content instruction.

In our implementation of coaching, we[1] found that when implemented systematically, coaching provides high-quality, ongoing professional learning if it is grounded on research-based instructional strategies, such as the ones described in this book, that make sense to teachers. Coaches guide and support teachers as they implement purposeful and rigorous language and literacy instruction side by side with core content matter.

Today, we regard coaching as a necessary part of any professional development workshop or comprehensive institute we offer. Having designed virtual coaching, schools now have options for implementing coaching. The *benefits of virtual coaching* are that (a) it doesn't disrupt the students in the classroom (the teachers place the camera in a strategic place or carry it when they want coaches to listen to their students' discourse), (b) it saves transition time for coaches and teachers, (c) the teacher and coach have more flexible locations for the feedback session, and (d) it saves schools money by reducing travel to workshops or institutes. What is captured by the camera is as close to an objective rendering of what actually transpires during the observation as one can achieve. The goals of both virtual and in-person coaching for teachers with MLs remain fundamentally the same.

1"We" refers to the fourteen independent consultants who are part of Margarita Calderón & Associates.

The Roles and Goals of Coaching

Coaching roles and the tasks assigned to multilingual/multiliteracy coaches (ML coaches) vary widely even in the same district. Some coaches support the implementation of multilingual instructional models or curricula, while others also must work to improve general instructional practices such as discipline and time on task. Some programs employ part-time coaches who work in one or more schools, while other full-time coaches might be placed in a single school. School districts sometimes employ full-time coaches to work with several schools.

The role of ML coaches has not been clearly defined in many cases. They might coach teachers who have MLs and others who do not. The lack of clearly defined roles and responsibilities for coaches can be a significant challenge. For example, often they are pulled away to assist with administrative tasks or for substitute teaching (Brown et al., 2006).

Killion et al. (2020) identify the roles for a typical coach shown in Figure 1.3. The brief descriptions in the right-hand column are my adaptations that align with ML coaches' roles.

Figure 1.3 Multilingual/Multiliteracy Coaches' Roles

KILLION'S ROLES OF COACHES	SAME ROLES ADAPTED BY MULTILINGUAL/MULTILITERACY COACHES
1. Data coach	The ML coach collects ethnographic and quantitative data with protocols for each component (vocabulary, discourse, reading, writing, social-emotional learning, content processing), shows data to teachers, and helps to analyze student performance and learning progressions to enact necessary adjustments.
2. Resource provider	The ML coach brings ancillary materials that relate to the component the teacher will teach for the observation.
3. Mentor	The ML coach mentors new school coaches.
4. Curriculum specialist	The ML coach meets with teachers in teacher learning communities to review and enhance curriculum.
5. Instructional specialist	The ML coach helps to adapt and integrate language, literacy, and social-emotional learning into lessons and to scaffold strategies for students with different levels of English proficiencies.
6. Classroom supporter	The ML coach models multilingual strategies and co-teaches with content, ESL, and special education teachers. The ML coach also monitors MLs while the teacher is teaching and helps MLs when necessary.
7. Learning facilitator	The ML coach facilitates learning by the ten roles listed here and by coaching teachers. The ML coach participates in teacher learning communities and conducts professional learning workshops.

(Continued)

(Continued)

KILLION'S ROLES OF COACHES	SAME ROLES ADAPTED BY MULTILINGUAL/MULTILITERACY COACHES
8. School leader	The ML coach is part of the leadership team in most schools and/or with the district administration and helps make important decisions for the multilingual program or makes recommendations.
9. Catalyst for change	The ML coach participates in leadership committees and contributes multilingual information and ideas for school plans and individual student plans. The ML coach strives to sustain the program quality and enhance attention, commitment, and knowledge on MLs.
10. Learner	ML coaches had to learn or amplify their knowledge, disposition, and skills to take on the role. Subsequently, continuous, intensive learning takes place when working with a diverse group of teachers, administrators, assessment specialists, psychologist, and others who are also learning about MLs.
	Some ML coaches assist with language proficiency testing of MLs once a year. They do or assist with data analyses and compliance reports for the school leadership, district, state, and federal agencies.
	ML coaches meet with other schools' coaches and expert coaches to reflect and continue to improve their practice.
	If ML coaches are bilingual, they are often called to translate for the families.
	See all features with the "What Coaches Do" label throughout this publication.

ESL Teachers as ML Coaches

Some ESL-trained coaches work directly with ESL teachers. At times, ESL teachers become the ESL coaches for other teachers. ESL coaches and ML coaches carry a double load. They support ESL teachers and their content co-teachers by helping articulate lesson designs, planning, and providing mini-workshops; organizing and managing the distribution of ML materials; administering language proficiency assessments to MLs; analyzing and maintaining data; meeting with and advising administrators; preparing compliance reports; and coaching if there is time. They have been known to do substantial substitute teaching. Additionally, they may be the official or unofficial translators in a school and/or the family liaisons. The ESL coaches deserve a medal! And a trophy! And a raise! At minimum, they merit the reduction of duties that do not pertain to the task of coaching teachers.

Figure 1.4   Goals of ML Coaching

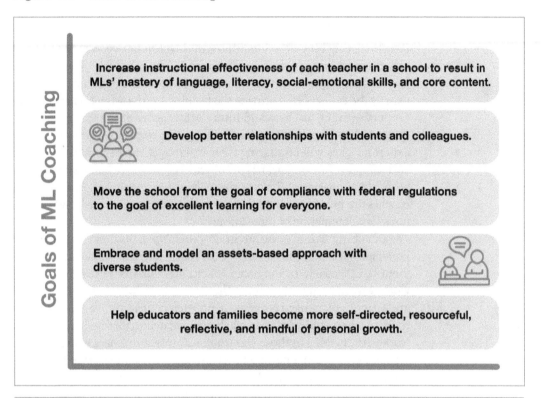

Source: Graphic by Nanci Esparza

 Available for download at http://resources.corwin.com/CMLExcellence

Similarities and Differences Between Coaching Models

Although most coaching programs share similar goals (Figure 1.4) and observation cycles, the philosophical approach varies. The ML coaching that we refer to in this book is different from other types of general class-room coaching. For example, Cognitive Coaching (Costa & Garmston, 2015) is different from the multilingual model of coaching, which is more similar to what Knight (2018) and Aguilar (2016; Bright Morning, 2024) propose.

As you will perceive in this book, the ML coaching cycle allows teach-ers to self-direct their learning by choosing a specific practice for vocabu-lary, reading, and/or writing instruction. The distributive leadership role of the ML coach is a combination of (1) supporting implementation of a second-language model, (2) improving one-on-one instructional prac-tices, and (3) helping to meet compliance or attain excellence with mul-tilingual assessments, recordkeeping, and reporting to local, state, and federal agencies.

Types of Coaching in Multilingual Schools

Excellent coaching relationships can develop between school-based coaches and outside-of-school *expert ML coaches* who specialize in second-language acquisition and multiple-literacies pedagogy. They are usually the trainers who provide the training for the school. They develop rapport with the teachers and future ML coaches at the workshops and discuss what the coaching will look like for the remainder of the year. Our expert coaches will be sharing their insights at the beginning or end of each chapter. One of the goals of the expert coach is to build capacity in a school by preparing and mentoring *school-based coaches*. School-based coaches are pivotal in sustaining the enthusiasm, refinement, and continuous implementation of innovations.

Coaching can also occur in *co-teaching situations* between the language specialist (often called ESL coach, English language development [ELD] coach, or language coach) and classroom teacher as they work toward a mutual goal for their students. Some schools/districts are assigning language coaches or *literacy coaches* to work with classroom teachers to support the teacher's instruction directed to MLs or to work with the MLs in those classrooms. Content teachers who are going through professional development workshops on integrating language, literacy, and content can also engage in *peer coaching* to support each other as they strive to learn and implement new teaching skills. Peer coaching is often called *collegial coaching*, which occurs in teacher learning communities (TLCs), first designed during the implementation of a dual-language program (Calderón, 1991). TLCs are similar to any collegial teams or DuFour and DuFour's (2012) professional learning communities (PLCs) in that they are places and spaces where after a workshop, book study, or conference teachers get together to make meaning, share ideas and strategies, solve problems of implementation, and celebrate student successes. Chapter 6 provides more specifics on TLCs. *Administrators as coaches* embrace a similar process. Despite being controversial, maneuvering differing opinions, and facing difficulties of implementation, administrators as coaches of teachers with MLs have been beneficial because administrators learn to apply ML coaching strategies in ML classrooms (Calderón, 2011). Students can also become *student peer coaches* as they work in project-based learning such as science, technology, engineering, the arts, and mathematics (STEAM) or even during smaller endeavors such as mastery of a word, clarifying a reading passage, or summarizing a paragraph.

Some coaching models offer teachers more autonomy while others are more directive. Some look for a balance between accountability and autonomy (Aguilar, 2018; Knight, 2018). Coaching in multilingual multicultural classrooms calls for a balance between the two. This balance will be visited in each chapter with the observation protocol and further details. We will give examples of how the model balances teacher choice and accountability.

What Multilingual Coaches Can Do

At a micro level, multilingual coaching programs are more structured than general education coaching programs due to the nature of the topics: observing language development in the context of discourse, the application of reading comprehension and text-based writing strategies, and social-emotional learning (SEL) integrated into the subjects that teachers are teaching. For example, a coach uses an observation protocol focusing only on the subcomponents that were presented at the workshop.

The observation protocols for each component are concise summaries of the key instructional strategies. These serve not only for the coaches to zoom in on their observations and give valuable feedback but also for teachers to remember the sequence and key pieces of a strategy as they plan a lesson. Thus, the teacher selects and informs the coach of the type of feedback desired. This will be better illustrated in each of the chapters as the instructional steps and the observation protocol are described.

Accountability and Support

After a quality professional development program, the transfer of that learning must be made visible so everyone can see what is being implemented, what is working, and what needs to be fixed. Coaches have a caring gentle way of observing and moving a project forward through four phases and purposes for coaching:

1. Quality preparation for coaching

2. Implementation of the innovation and coaching of that innovation

3. Support as teachers develop efficacy

4. Data analysis of MLs' learning progress

Coaching Systematic Content With Systematic Observations

Hattie and Timperley (2007) assert that there have been few studies about coaching, yet that feedback is one of the most powerful influences on learning and achievement. They point out that this impact can be either positive or negative. It depends on the circumstances that make it effective. We find this to be true when generic coaching is used to attempt to give feedback to teachers and the checklist they use is designed for things irrelevant to the model being implemented. *This might be the reason that many teachers are reluctant to participate in coaching: They find it irrelevant.* On the other hand, it becomes a positive experience when they see coaches participating with them in the workshops. This reassures them that they will speak the same language as they set up their preconference and when they discuss the data collected during the observation.

Why Your Current Coaching Model Might Not Work

Generic lists or any type of coaching that is not specific to teaching/learning academic vocabulary, reading comprehension, student interaction around the reading selection, and text-based writing *will not work* in classrooms with MLs. The observations and feedback must be distinctly focused on the integration of language and literacy with content and how that affects student learning. The diverse levels of English proficiencies in a classroom are one of the greatest challenges for unprepared coaches.

Unsystematic content. Along with the one-shot workshop, there is another trend that persists. The trend is to invite entertaining and motivating presenters. Motivation is good and necessary, but beyond that, teachers can apply very little in their classrooms. Unless the participants walk away knowing how to convert those emotions into instructional enhancements, they won't be able to apply them. In addition to excitable and renewal workshops, teachers need ideas and strategies that are explicitly described and modeled for a powerful implementation. The coaches attending such one-shot sessions will be nonplussed as to how to coach that. Follow-up workshops where modeling of strategies and discussions surround application will enhance the initial excitement.

Leadership messaging. Changing instructional practices to fit in vocabulary and reading comprehension is difficult enough; adding coaching duties on top of this becomes almost unbearable for some teachers, who end up avoiding both in order to cope. This is when the principal of the school should reinforce the message that (1) coaching carries benefits for all teachers, both seasoned and new; (2) accommodating practices to promote vocabulary development and reading comprehension are "not just another thing to pile on your plate," but essential bridges to content mastery; and (3) engaging in these practices is not just the responsibility of a select few but an expectation for everyone at the school.

Systematic content. Knight and colleagues (2020) affirmed that an instructional playbook makes learning real. Instructional playbooks are organizational tools that professional developers use to "(1) identify high-impact teaching strategies and (2) explain those strategies to teachers so they and their students can meet powerful goals" (Knight et al., 2020, p. 141). The bulleted list under the "Coaches Address Context and Components" heading (page 00) gives a glimpse into an evidence-based instructional playbook for coaches and teachers working with MLs. Each high-impact component is based on the ExC-ELL model and described in Chapters 3, 4, and 5.

An instructional playbook must be part of the professional development workshops. Additionally, another playbook for site administrators is a way to have all the messages, roles, commitments, teacher support systems, and goals always on hand.

A playbook for ML coaches is necessary since they may be new to instruction of MLs and lack sufficient background knowledge and skills to address the diverse social-emotional, academic, linguistic, and cultural needs of MLs. This book was written to be such a playbook for coaches.

---

1. What main differences do you see between a coaching model used at your school and classroom coaching of MLs?

2. What will be your first step in this personal rewarding journey?

What Coaches Do to Prepare for What Could Be Excellence

ML coaches want to prepare for continuous learning and be recognized as professional learning leaders. If they can influence not just participants' professional practice but participants' sense of agency about changing their practice, they can cultivate habits that lead to a continuous learning culture that will impact MLs for the rest of their lives.

The following twelve ExC-ELL components and pedagogical supports are used as examples of evidence-based instruction tested with MLs. Each is described throughout the chapters to serve as examples of what your school/district might want to adopt.

What Is ExC-ELL?

Expediting Comprehension for English Language Learners (ExC-ELL) is an evidence-based whole-school professional learning model for K–12 teachers, coaches, and administrators.

The process consists of several days of professional learning that combine (1) evidence-based research and framework presentation; (2) modeling and practice of instructional strategies for vocabulary,

(Continued)

(Continued)

discourse, reading, and writing integrated into content areas; (3) peer practice with strategies; (4) lesson application; (5) follow-up coaching; and (6) teacher learning communities (TLCs).

As an ExC-ELL coach, you will assist, facilitate, model, observe, collect data, give feedback, and jointly plan for the twelve components:

1. Teaching of vocabulary

2. Knowledge building

3. Oral discourse throughout the lesson

4. Modeling reading comprehension strategies

5. Partner reading + summarizing

6. Depth of word study

7. Close reading

8. Cooperative learning strategies

9. Drafting

10. Editing and revising

11. Conclusions and titles

12. Multimodal assessment practices

Undergirding the twelve components are the sociocultural and student-centered ways to leverage students' linguistic and cultural capital. Social-emotional competencies are taught in the context of a learning event/activity.

Coaches Address Context and Components

▶ Create a safe context for MLs to listen, speak, read, verbally analyze and synthesize, and write.

▶ Simultaneously support and challenge teachers.

- Leverage students' cultural capital.

- Foster learning of social-emotional competencies—self-management, self-awareness, social-awareness, relationship skills, and responsible decision making.

- Coach vocabulary as a precursor to reading, for processing information, for intentional incidental word teaching, and for writing.

- Coach discourse, encouraging frequency and quality of interaction and continuous use of new words and sentence structures by MLs.

- Coach reading—fluency and comprehension, applying critical thinking, content mastery, and connections to students' own lives and others.

- Coach writing—drafting, editing, revising strategies for MLs, and helping the teacher to reflect on final student products.

- Coach performance assessment—assessing use of vocabulary in the context of interaction during partner practice; partner reading; partner summaries; cooperative learning; project-based learning; science, technology, engineering, and mathematics (STEM); presentations; and reading comprehension and composition.

- Assist in the development of social-emotional competencies, linguistically and culturally responsive teaching and learning integrated into each subcomponent, and the classroom management that values student background, languages, and literacies.

- Have courageous conversations around bias, stereotyping, trauma, relationship building, and classroom and school structures that accelerate success for MLs and their classroom peers.

What Coaches Do to Address All Components

We break up learning into small chunks for better student processing. We can do the same for teachers.

Since the list of twelve ExC-ELL components is a comprehensive language and literacy model for core content classrooms, a strong recommendation is to break up the list for implementation.

For example, after a workshop on selecting and teaching vocabulary, teachers and coaches can concentrate solely on the implementation of vocabulary. Parsing (Figure 1.5) helps to better analyze what works and where more work is needed on each component. It might take several months to complete the twelve-component cycle and attend to all teachers. It is understood that some teachers might need more assistance than others.

After conquering vocabulary, the next cycle would consist of a professional development session on discourse and reading. Coaching would be on discourse and reading comprehension strategies only for at least a semester. The reading component is the most challenging for content teachers. That might need revisiting with another workshop or more coaching.

Lesson preparation for reading means not only selecting words that will be most useful for MLs to enter that text but also selecting sentence structures that are inherent to that subject area. The way we speak and write in mathematics is very different from the way we do so in science or in English language arts. Social-emotional competencies and norms of interaction can be learned concomitantly with each component and each instructional routine and strategy. Performance assessment would also be part of each component as the teacher observes, annotates, and analyzes student discourse and products. The observation protocol is also chunked into each component.

MYTH

High school teachers are not reading teachers.

Key Roles and Soft Skills

Coaching offers a safe place to think, to reflect, to speak truthfully, and to ask questions—about self and others (Kee et al., 2010).

The role of school administrators. Principals can make or break a coaching program. Principals, assistant principals, coordinators, family facilitators, and psychologists must attend all workshops with the

Figure 1.5 Parsing the Professional Development Delivery

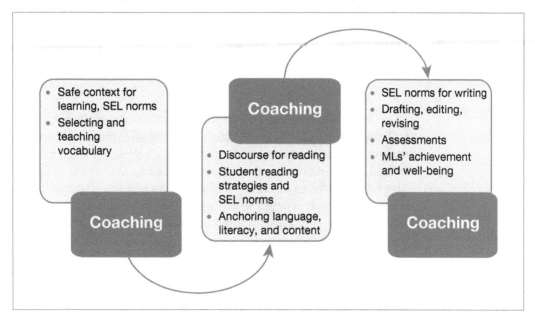

Source: Adapted from Zacarian et al. (2021).

online resources Available for download at http://resources.corwin.com/CMLExcellence

teachers and participate in a special session on how to support the teachers as they go through the implementation's highs and lows. Principals are also invited to use the observation protocol and practice coaching teachers. An exciting offshoot is that they often use those strategies to ascertain a more accurate picture when it's time to evaluate teachers.

Teacher autonomy and accountability. Teachers want to be self-directed and free to make their own decisions and choices. Yet, teachers are being asked to shift in ways where they might not have much of a say-so. When teachers resist innovations, there can be many reasons. One of those is feeling they have no say in the coaching relationship. Transformation for individuals and organizations remains a daunting and complex proposition (Costa & Garmston, 2015). Bringing languages and cultures into an already complex situation becomes quite challenging for the coach who has not experienced such a context before. *Coaches will need special skills to work with the diversity of teacher dispositions, beliefs, biases, and values about multilingual diversity.* Coaches demonstrate to teachers they are on the same page when they attend workshops with the teachers where they learn more about MLs' diversity and assets. As they learn together at the workshops, coaches also begin to develop relationships with the teachers. Knight (2021) discusses five stages of teacher implementation as seen in Figure 1.6. The teacher–coach relationship acknowledges these stages as a normal path to success and to map out their plan.

Figure 1.6   Five Stages of Teacher Implementation

We can assume that you will run into a diversity of teaching skills and dispositions. These stages imply levels of skill, fears, and willingness to try. You will encounter teachers whose beliefs, biases, and uninformed misconceptions about language and cultural diversity are deep. Bruce Joyce used to say that there will always be the 10 percent who resist; therefore, it is better to concentrate on the 90 percent (Calderón & Marsh, 1989). For many, it is merely helping to overcome fears—once they are identified!

Coaches partner with teachers to identify, explain, model, and adapt teaching strategies so teachers and students can meet their goals (Knight, 2022).

Having faith in all teachers. We believe that all teachers have the desire to be their best and have the capacity to learn throughout their professional lifespans. We believe that once teachers begin to see the changes in students, they become believers in the innovation. Hence, this is the reason to gently stay with them. When the whole school is participating, the students are the first to embrace and appreciate the changes. They will ask teachers to use the strategy that "our science teacher is using for vocabulary" or ask to "read with a buddy the way we do in social studies."

Coaches' well-being. Coaches need coaches. The district must enact coaches' learning communities (CLCs) where they can exchange ideas, successes, and problem solving. All coaches will also be learning the new instructional strategies and how to observe, document, and give feedback based on objective data. This shared learning will accelerate quality implementation and success for everyone.

Here are some ideas for a coach new to multilingual/multicultural observations:

▶ Attend the workshops with the teachers to better understand how coaching this innovation works best.

▶ View videos of the training to review and delve deeper.

▶ Video record yourself during feedback sessions. Study your spoken language and body language.

- Reread this book. Share this book with colleagues to study with you.

- Visit a seasoned ESL/ELD teacher to practice observing and giving feedback.

- Have ongoing conversations about how the innovation or implementation meets individual teachers' and students' needs, and where adaptations are necessary.

- Create a psychologically safe place for your coaching conversations.

- Value your relationship with all teachers.

- Never lose sight that teachers need you and appreciate your support.

Effort is a factor that has to be consistent with one's personal motivation and committed goals. Further, it is tied to one's self-efficacy level or confidence that we can succeed (Hattie & Yates, 2014).

Flexible Delivery and Scheduling Are a Must

Coaches conduct instructional coaching cycles through observations, reflection on data gathered, actionable feedback, and jointly determining the next steps. They avoid looking for unrelated features to the component being observed and concentrate on the agreed-upon feature and time frame requested by the teacher.

Coaching doesn't have to be only in person anymore. More schools are preferring virtual coaching. There are two ways to do virtual coaching. For instance, a teacher can upload a video to a Swivl Cloud where a coach can provide feedback on that site. Swivl provides a reflectivity device that can hold a camera, phone, or tablet situated in the back of the room to follow the teacher's movement. The teacher wears a microphone to record themselves and students close by. The video can be shared with the coach during the feedback/analysis session or on a cloud for the coach or teacher to review before they meet. The teacher has the option to make the site private or share.

Virtual coaching can be implemented by using Zoom or Google Meet to observe a teacher for fifteen minutes. During another fifteen minutes, the coach presents the data to the teacher, helps reflect on the data, and gives feedback. The teacher and coach plan immediate action steps, selecting one or two ways in which the teacher can enhance practice and prepare for the next coaching observation.

The following tips and tools are scripts that the ExC-ELL professional development program consultants send to their schools to prepare for each observation.

What Coaches Do to Support Scheduling

Coaches can help set up the best configuration for the school. Since there are benefits to both in-person and virtual coaching, the coach and administration should consult with teachers for the final decision. Here are some tools that coaches use for either in-person or virtual ExC-ELL coaching.

In-Person Coaching Options

Several options for in-person coaching situations are available for schools or teachers to choose. The following email is an example of how to inform principals and teachers about their options.

Example of the Email Sent to the Principal

Since we will soon visit your school, we would like to offer the following coaching options for your teachers to select one and inform us ahead of time which one they select. Some of these options require more preparation on our part; therefore, it is crucial that we have the information outlined as follows.

Options for 30-Minute Blocks of In-Person Coaching

1. An ExC-ELL coach observes a teacher implementing a strategy, selected by the teacher (e.g., partner reading, Numbered Heads Together, a roundtable, or a Cut 'n' Grow [see Chapter 5; Calderón, 1984, 1986, 1990, 1994, 1996]), and gives feedback afterward. The teacher selects the focus of the observation.

2. The teacher introduces a lesson, and an ExC-ELL coach demonstrates a strategy with the students. They debrief the lesson afterward.

3. An ExC-ELL coach observes students applying a strategy as the teacher conducts a lesson (e.g., seven-step vocabulary, partner

reading, or summarization [Calderón, 1984, 1986, 1990, 1994, 1996]), and then the coach observes and collects information on the students' application.

4. During a 30-minute ExC-ELL team meeting, one or two teachers share a 5-minute strategy that has worked for them, and three or four other teachers ask questions or add other success stories.

5. An ExC-ELL coach helps a teacher develop or refine a lesson.

6. Instructional walk-throughs occur where classrooms are visited for 10 minutes by a team of five or six teachers and the ExC-ELL coach. The focus can be on an ExC-ELL strategy, classroom management, or student interaction.

7. Peer coaching: If two teachers want to observe each other and give each other feedback, an ExC-ELL coach will show them the protocol for peer coaching, giving constructive feedback, and setting goals.

8. The coach attends a TLC/PLC if teachers invite the coach to attend to answer questions or model a strategy.

9. Action research occurs where a teacher studies an aspect of the students' learning by recording their performance over a certain period. The ExC-ELL coach can provide guidelines or research suggestions for this study.

Logistical Information to Help the Coaches Prepare

▶ Please submit the schedule for observations/coaching options and time for debriefing/planning with the teacher.

▶ We can typically observe five or six teachers during 20- to 30-minute intervals (5 minutes to get to the next classroom). We will need at least 20 minutes to debrief or plan with each teacher afterward.

▶ If there is time at the end of the day or another convenient time for us to do a "Refresher Workshop" for 45 to 60 minutes, please indicate on the schedule.

▶ If co-teaching of a lesson has been selected, please send copies of the portion of the text the students will be reading and the intended lesson plan.

(Continued)

(Continued)

▶ If instructional rounds have been selected by five or six teachers, make sure you identify the classrooms these teachers will visit for 10 minutes. We can meet with the group first thing in the morning to plan the focus of the rounds.

▶ Please send us the completed "Day Schedule" a week before, using an organizer such as the following [see Figure 1.7]:

Figure 1.7   Coaching Day Schedule

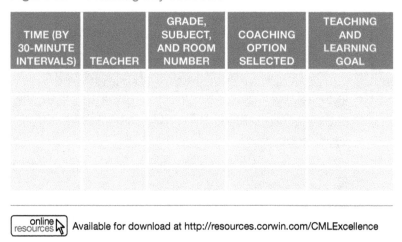

TIME (BY 30-MINUTE INTERVALS)	TEACHER	GRADE, SUBJECT, AND ROOM NUMBER	COACHING OPTION SELECTED	TEACHING AND LEARNING GOAL

online resources   Available for download at http://resources.corwin.com/CMLExcellence

Example of Flexible Virtual Coaching

Using a cloud-based platform like Google Drive or Microsoft OneDrive, a principal can share a sign-up sheet for virtual coaching to which teachers can add their names in real time (see Figure 1.8). The sign-up sheet can also include a hotlink to a Tips for Coaching Day document for teachers to review as they prepare for their observation. Once they have selected the time for their observation, the coaches will place a link to their virtual meeting space (using Zoom, Google Meet, or a similar service) directly onto the coaching sign-up sheet as well. This provides teachers, coaches, and the principal with a one-stop document where they can find all the information they need for a coaching day.

On the coaching day, the coach will check the sign-up sheet for any adjustments. Both teachers and coaches will know exactly what to expect. For example, after a workshop on preteaching vocabulary, fifteen-minute observations are sufficient to observe a teacher teach five words using the seven-step strategy described in Chapter 4. Another fifteen minutes afterward will be sufficient for reflection, feedback, and jointly determining goals for enhancement.

Example of Form Sent to Principals for Planning Virtual Visits

Hello again,

Let's get ready for your school's coaching day on writing strategies! Below please find the link to the sign-up sheet for your ExC-ELL coaching day for writing on April 11. Each teacher will sign up for *two* time slots: a 15-minute observation and a 15-minute feedback session with the same coach later in the day.

You are free to assign teachers to participate in coaching, or to let teachers volunteer; either way, though, we do ask that you ensure that no more than 16 teachers total sign up: up to 8 with each coach.

We also encourage you to let teachers know about the Tips for Coaching Day document that can be found on the sign-up sheet. This short document answers most teachers' questions about coaching and can be very helpful as teachers prepare to be observed.

Finally, we look forward to your teachers participating in coaching! We receive a lot of positive feedback about ExC-ELL professional development, but the *most positive* feedback we receive is from teachers who received one-on-one support from one of our coaches. It is a powerful experience!

Please let me know if you have any questions or if there is anything else I can do for you!

Here's the link to your coaching sign-up sheet for April 11.

:) Leticia

Figure 1.8   Example Coaching Sign-Up Sheet for Virtual Coaching

TIMES	STEP 1	STEP 2	STEP 3	STEP 4	STEP 5
	ADD your name, grade level, or subject area in TWO places.	CHOOSE observation or feedback. (Make sure to sign up for both!)	READ the "Tips for Coaching Day." Have a plan for how you will share your classroom virtually (laptop, webcam, etc.).	CHECK that you read the "Tips for Coaching Day."	On coaching day, JOIN the Zoom link below.
8:00		▼	Tips for Coaching Day		[link]

(Continued)

(Continued)

TIMES	STEP 1	STEP 2	STEP 3	STEP 4	STEP 5
8:15		▼	Tips for Coaching Day		[link]
8:30		▼	Tips for Coaching Day		[link]
8:45		▼	Tips for Coaching Day		[link]
9:00		▼	Tips for Coaching Day		[link]
9:15		▼	Tips for Coaching Day		[link]

Options for Reporting

Reports can be valuable or quite controversial. Teachers need to know if the coaching information will be shared with the administration. They do not want surprises or to feel that "Big Brother" is out to get them. Three options for reporting or not reporting feedback results to the administration after a coaching session can be explained at the joint professional workshop, and the administration must be explicit as to which they will embrace: (1) Some school administrators request reports after every coaching visit for each teacher as a summary of what was observed, what was working, and next steps for the school. This option is usually preferred when a school is out of compliance with the Office for Civil Rights. (2) On the other hand, many administrators do not request reports because they feel that coaching and feedback are private explorations/conversations between coach and teacher. (3) Still others, with the teacher's permission, request the results of the observation protocol and notes for filing purposes but not as reports or evaluations. The files serve as part of a teacher's portfolio for advancement or stipends as part of their continuous on-the-job learning.

What Coaches Do to Change Schools for Better ML Outcomes

Hargreaves and Fullan (2012) discuss the importance of teacher development to effect change in schools. Change is to be expected when professional development and coaching are systematic and the whole school participates. We delight in schools that are willing to implement a comprehensive model. Due to the COVID-19 slowdown, many schools are actively seeking changes. When your school is ready to embrace change, it will become much easier to integrate evidence-based instructional practices for MLs.

Barth (1990) proposed that everyone can be learning simultaneously—teachers, students, administrators. A school where everyone learns also wins because it becomes an ecology of reflection, growth, and refinement of practice. It builds the type of mindsets necessary for change. When we contemplate what has happened since the onset of the COVID-19 pandemic, and the disappointing results from reading, mathematics, and social studies national tests, it is easier to agree that change is necessary. When we think of the increase of multilingual students and other newcomers arriving in every school, it is easier to consider what changes need to take place.

"Coaching that's aligned to a comprehensive professional development plan enables the learner to go deep and wide into a content area, instructional practice, or particular aspect of teaching. And it facilitates alignment between everyone responsible for building a teacher's capacity" (Aguilar, 2014).

What Is Yet to Be in Every School

A whole-school approach to professional development and coaching builds capacity and positive attitudes toward all students and ensures school improvement.

MYTH

MLs are the responsibility of ESL teachers.

Moving away from "those are the ESL teacher's students" to "all students are my responsibility, and I will learn" is a strong indicator of whole-school commitment and improvement. The social organization of "us and them" shifts to "we're in the same boat, and we won't let it sink."

What Coaches Do to Sustain Momentum: Teacher Learning Communities

As a complementary follow-up to coaching, teachers and coaches meet once a week for ongoing inquiry, collaboration, and reflective dialogue in teacher learning communities (TLCs). The teacher participants become collegial coaches in TLCs. When a teacher wants feedback on a strategy that worked or needs fine-tuning, the others act as coaches and give specific feedback. TLCs are similar to PLCs but concentrate on MLs' progress and success. Modeling and conversations are key to clarifying and negotiating quality implementation. Sometimes just having opportunities to talk with peers results in great ideas for anchoring implementation. Participating teachers assess students' artifacts, adjust lessons, and refine the internalization process to achieve the desired literacy outcomes to meet the needs of all MLs (Calderón, 1991). Coaches can be on hand when teachers request additional assistance.

What Coaches Do to Help Whole-School Implementation

Why help enact comprehensive professional development with follow-up coaching? There are many benefits.

1. Everyone in the school (expert and novice; ESL/ELD and general education teachers) is in the same boat learning something new.

2. All work toward the same goal.

3. Reduces isolation.

4. Builds a common language.

5. Forges respect for diversity.

6. Refined as it continues to be implemented.

7. Helps to make decisions that will affect everyone positively.

8. Mindsets shift to examine own attitudes, beliefs, biases, and practices.

9. Everyone is a staff developer for everyone else.

10. Helps everyone discover their own talents and strengths.

Barriers to Anticipate for a Quality Coaching Implementation

1. Time constraints

2. Complexity of the subject matter

3. Fear of change

4. Personal beliefs about MLs

5. The problem of generalizing versus differentiating

6. Interpersonal and school political problems

7. Legal compliance

> We all fall short of being who we want to be at times. We think/ say things about others that are dehumanizing. We don't listen. We ask leading questions. We stumble through feedback. All this is normal. What is exceptional is our desire and commitment to do better (Bright Morning, 2024; accessed June 5, 2023).

For a coach and teacher to arrive at their goals, good conditions for adult learning must be established. The foundation is the professional development program design and implementation.

There are too many times when a quality professional development program doesn't work. Large amounts of money, time, and effort are spent to initiate, but there is little of all that in the follow-up to the initial workshops. In terms of cost, the follow-up coaching is approximately 75 percent of a professional learning program. It is the school site coaching and collegial continuation of refinement after expert coaches leave that makes a difference for teachers and for students. Figures 1.9 and 1.10 compare what works and what doesn't. They are reminders for planning a comprehensive approach versus "just workshops" that do not make a difference.

Figure 1.9 Professional Learning: What It Is and What It Isn't

WHAT PROFESSIONAL LEARNING IS *NOT*	WHAT PROFESSIONAL LEARNING *IS*
Only one workshop is held on the topic.	Workshops occur throughout the year as part of a three-year plan.
No coaching follows on what was presented in the workshop(s).	Coaching is provided after each component that was presented at workshops.
Workshops are on the flavor-of-the-month topics or one-shot events from popular presenters.	Systematic cohesive sessions address each component in depth.
Feelgood workshops motivate but leave little to implement and have no impact on student achievement.	Each workshop presents theory, research, demonstrations of the strategies, and ways to apply and integrate them into existing requirements and lessons.
Only a small percentage of the instructional staff attend, and they are expected to share with the rest of the school staff (which rarely occurs).	The whole teaching staff, coordinators, counselors, directors, assistant principals, and principals attend all sessions.
Instructional programs/strategies are deemed ineffective because they were not implemented, and another instructional model is brought in to try instead.	Teachers participate in weekly teacher learning communities (TLCs) for collaborative learning and quality adaptation.

(Continued)

(Continued)

WHAT PROFESSIONAL LEARNING IS *NOT*	WHAT PROFESSIONAL LEARNING *IS*
Only a small percentage of the budget is spent on professional learning—and it is mostly for going to conferences.	A large percentage of the budget is spent on site-based professional workshops, TLCs, and coaching every teacher after each component that builds upon the other and teacher incentives.
Instead of professional development, teachers opt for learning communities where knowledge remains stagnant.	Teachers in learning communities are avid searchers of evidence-based knowledge to enhance their practices.

Source: Adapted from Calderón & Tartaglia (2023).

 Available for download at http://resources.corwin.com/CMLExcellence

Figure 1.10   Systematic Coaching

WHAT COACHING IS *NOT*	WHAT COACHING *IS*
A one-shot for each teacher	Consistent coaching is provided on each chunk of a comprehensive framework.
Using a generic observation checklist with many items to check	Each observation has a specific observation protocol.
Using an observation protocol that has not been empirically tested for validity and reliability with MLs	The observation protocol was tested for validity and reliability including teams of central and school administrators, ESL/ELD teachers, and general education/core content teachers.
Walking into a classroom unannounced	The coaching session involves either a teacher-selected component or a preconference with a teacher, based on an understanding and agreement of what is to be observed for 15 minutes.
Staying in a classroom for long periods of time to catch something "good" or "useful for giving advice"	An agreed-upon 15-minute observation focuses on teacher and student performance on a particular strategy.
Submitting feedback days later when its impact is no longer as useful	Coaches submit to teachers (and their principal if that is the agreement) written reports of each observation and the school's progress by the next day.

 Available for download at http://resources.corwin.com/CMLExcellence

Recently, there has been a push to move from offering professional development workshops to only instituting PLCs (Brock, 2023), but the comparative research with outcomes between professional development–coaching–TLCs and PLCs only has yet to emerge. Professional development has had a bad rap because it usually doesn't include coaching or TLCs/PLCs. Professional development or professional learning can still work if some trends that render it unsatisfactory can be done away with and it becomes a comprehensive approach with extensive follow-up. Here are some tips to help sustain that comprehensiveness.

Reflections

1. How many "What Learning *Is*" and how many "What Learning Is *Not*" components (Figure 1.9) are prevalent in your school?

2. How many "What Coaching *Is*" and how many "What Coaching Is *Not*" components (Figure 1.10) undergird the dominant tradition in your school?

3. How much of the budget is allocated to coaching?

4. How often can you, as a coach, organize a meeting with the school leadership to discuss some next steps?

Figure 1.11 is a tool for leadership teams to discuss the enactment of the professional development model and to gauge what is in place, what is in progress, and what has been accomplished.

Figure 1.11   Coaches Help to Guide the Conversations in Collegial Teams

QUALITY FEATURES OF OUR PROFESSIONAL DEVELOPMENT	IN PLACE	WE ARE WORKING ON:	WE NEED TO:
Coaching is provided after each component that was presented at workshops.			
Systematic cohesive sessions address each component in depth.			

(Continued)

(Continued)

QUALITY FEATURES OF OUR PROFESSIONAL DEVELOPMENT	IN PLACE	WE ARE WORKING ON:	WE NEED TO:
Each workshop presents research, modeling of the strategies, and ways to apply and integrate them into existing requirements and lessons.			
The whole teaching staff, coordinators, counselors, directors, assistant principals, and principals attend all sessions.			
Teachers participate in weekly teacher learning communities (TLCs) for quality adaptation and more collegial learning.			
A large percentage of the budget is spent on site-based professional workshops, TLCs, and coaching every teacher after each component.			
Consistent coaching is provided on each chunk of a comprehensive framework.			

online resources 🔖 Available for download at http://resources.corwin.com/CMLExcellence

What Coaches Do for Coaches

Coaches' Learning Communities (CLCs). Having opportunities to discuss with other coaches what's going on and new ideas and to reflect is important because individuals clarify and negotiate meaning during conversations. These conversations are very important for students and teachers, as previously mentioned, but more so for coaches. Coaches also need opportunities to reflect, plan, renew enthusiasm, and celebrate with peers (see Figure 1.12). Ideally, the school district includes in their plans opportunities for coaches to study their craft with peer coaches.

Figure 1.12 Coaches' Learning Communities

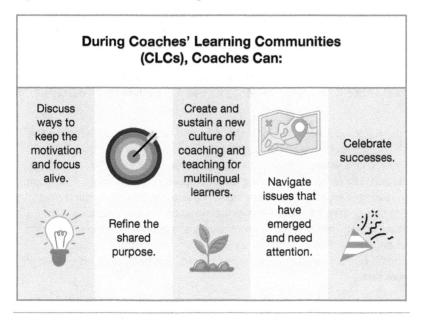

Source: Graphic by Leticia M. Trower

online resources ➘ Available for download at http://resources.corwin.com/CMLExcellence

When possible, coaches might want to visit Jim Knight's instructional coaching site (https://www.instructionalcoaching.com) or attend workshops such as "The Art of Coaching" by Elena Aguilar, about which you can find more information on her website (https://www.brightmorn ingteam.com) for additional learning. Coaches might also want to explore websites on teaching MLs such as www.exc-ell.com for resources and listings of ongoing workshops for whole-school professional development and coaching.

Message From a Special Guest: Data Coaches

By Margo Gottlieb

Coaching focuses on the development of knowledge and practice through a range of possible relational dynamics (Teemant & Sherman, 2022). Data coaching is a specialty that involves relationship building in the handling of student and school information to improve teaching and learning. That's where I come in . . . as an educator who has been dedicated to sharing equitable assessment practices for MLs with others her entire professional career.

Data coaches in schools and districts with MLs realize the importance of relationships as teachers, students, and families work together to spearhead change in assessment practices. As conveyers of a positive vision and advocates for this growing heterogeneous student population, these ambassadors guide teachers or PLCs in co-creating shared learning goals based on students' evidence for learning gathered from multiple sources.

For MLs, robust evidence for learning should represent assessment within a linguistic and culturally responsive curriculum. Easier said than done, right? That's where a data coach can be helpful. For example, for the last decade, I have been advocating for a comprehensive model for classroom assessment *as*, *for*, and *of* learning to replace the formative–summative dichotomy. Why? Because this model relies on the humanistic side of assessment—relationships—emphasizing the interaction among students, among students and teachers, as well as among teachers and school leaders rather than decontextualized scores, numbers, or levels generated from tests.

Aware of comprehensive and balanced assessment models that center on multilingual learners, data coaches must be sensitive and often ready to counteract policies and decisions that are predicated on large-scale standardized measures with often skewed results that carry negative consequences for MLs. Data coaches have the expertise to rely on relevant and useful information to inform teaching and learning.

Although data coaches may not be able to change the assessment landscape, they are positioned to make it more attractive and navigable for teachers and school leaders. Together data coaches and educators of MLs must keep all of the following in mind:

- Classroom data from MLs and MLs with exceptionalities along with their families and teachers should be systematically collected, analyzed, reported, and archived to serve as evidence for informing local decision making.

- Classroom data should stimulate teacher conversations on sensitive topics, such as the lived experiences and trauma of MLs, bias/stereotyping, and linguistic/cultural factors that contribute to student identities, to shape the context for interpretation.

- Classroom data, in conjunction with data from standardized measures with valid inferences for multilingual learners, when enacted in a linguistic and culturally responsive learning environment, should serve to accelerate student growth and goal attainment.

- Classroom data should spur ongoing actionable feedback to and from students and, when based on sound assessment practices coupled with guidance, move student learning forward.

- Classroom data should contribute to a data-informed school culture built around relationships and shared values—one in which both teachers and students can thrive. While not all schools or districts are fortunate enough to have data coaches, you can form a data team to collaborate in processing and communicating information across classrooms. As coaches of MLs, it is paramount that you act on what really counts—the relationships formed with students—to offer more equitable access, increased opportunities, and sound evidence to ensure their success.

Margo Gottlieb, PhD, is co-founder and lead developer of WIDA at the University of Wisconsin–Madison. Margo has multiple books on assessment and presents at national and international conferences.

From One Coach to Another

As I walked nervously into the fifth-grade classroom of Ms. K., I looked around the room and pictured all the students who would soon be sitting in the desks. I thought about all the laughs, the tears, and of course the learning. I glanced up behind Ms. K.'s desk and saw a huge 5K on the wall. I would later learn that she would explain to her class that she was like their coach alongside them as they learned and grew during their fifth-grade year. I instantly knew that she and I shared the same philosophy of teaching. As the year began, I was once again reminded of the deep level of grade-level content that MLs are expected to learn all while gaining English language proficiency. As a coach, I have the amazing opportunity to be a stakeholder in this process and work with both the teachers and the students. Coaching provides the opportunity for all teachers of MLs to understand, implement, and be supported in using

(Continued)

(Continued)

the strategies that are essential for MLs to meet the challenging content demands and develop English skills. Together coaches and teachers can also help MLs recognize that they are valued and welcomed in the classroom and in the entire school community. Walking alongside a teacher throughout this process provides a way for teachers to collaborate, advocate, and support our MLs, not only in the classroom, but also in society as they are becoming our future leaders.

—Alyson Reilly, Lead English for Speakers of Other Languages (ESOL) Teacher

What Do Instructional Coaches Need to Know to Coach Teachers With Multilingual Learners?

CHAPTER
#2

From One Coach to Another: Tips for Coaches of Teachers With Multilingual Learners

Coaching teachers of multilingual learners opens a door to continue supporting students who are at different levels of language acquisition with a specific focus on newly arrived students. As a newly arrived multilingual student at the high school level, I experienced the urgency to learn the language in meaningful ways and connect them to the context of my studies while applying it to reading and writing. When working with teachers, I try purposefully to make a connection with what students experience and with teachers; it is like teaching others to see things from various perspectives. By doing this, teachers find that our feedback conversation becomes more meaningful as examples are being brought up, and teachers are able to find the importance of carefully selecting words for the instructional experience. Furthermore, during this experience, teachers can connect the "why" of their lesson to vocabulary instruction and to opportunities to incorporate reading and writing strategies for a valuable learning experience. This provides learners with many opportunities to absorb the learning of words, in the right context, and manipulate new learning by applying various modalities ultimately to produce it in oral discourse, reading, and writing.

—Giuliana Jahnsen Lewis, Assistant Principal and (Former) Instructional Coach, Sterling Middle School

According to the U.S. Department of Education, there are over 5.3 million multilingual learners (MLs) in U.S. public schools. About 76 percent are Spanish speakers (National Center for Education Statistics [NCES], 2024). Although there are many language groups, Latino students will soon be 30 percent of all public school enrollment, and many of them will be MLs. Educators now prefer the term *multilingual learners* or *emergent bilinguals* to *English learners* or *emergent multilingual learners*. In addition to these popular labels, there are other terms to consider as you will see in Figure 2.1. Not surprisingly, some categories of MLs are not included in the 5.3 million count (NCES, 2024). All this means that your school most likely has or will have MLs and will need coaches who can assist teachers with quality learning and quality implementation of that learning.

MLs come from a variety of backgrounds. They bring a myriad of language practices, knowledge, values, worldviews, and conventions from their families, cultures, and communities.

Let's consider *multilingual* the umbrella term for this rich diversity. Under that umbrella, there will be variation in English proficiency, years of education or no education, knowledge of one or more languages, socioeconomic status, homelessness, refugee status, undocumented status, religion, and extraordinary survival strengths and worldly smarts.

Figure 2.1   The Diversity of Multilingual Learners

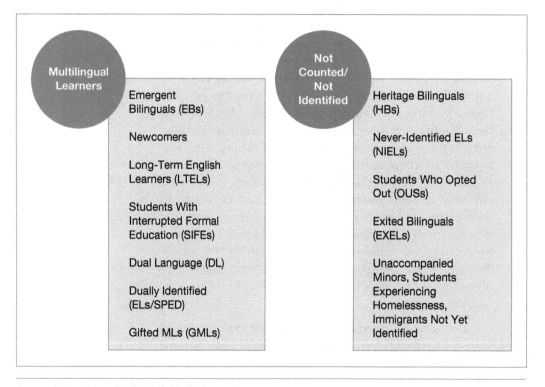

Source: Adapted from Gottlieb & Calderón (in press).

Multilingual Learners

There are many categories, interpretations, and terms for multilingual students. *English learners (ELs)* is the official term that the U.S. Departments of Justice and Education still use in their documents. *Multilingual learners (MLs)* is the term that educators prefer, as it accentuates the bilingual potential of students who navigate multilingual environments (Gottlieb & Calderón, in press). It is usually the broader umbrella term for all multilingual student categories. A teacher can have a room full of MLs—students who speak different languages and have different ethnicities—but only a handful may be officially identified as ELs. ELs are sometimes called *English language learners (ELLs)*. Some states like Texas prefer *emergent bilinguals (EBs)* in that the term is assets-based and encompasses all categories. A teacher might have two *newcomers* and will call them MLs or EBs. In some cases, the term *newcomers* will be used due to the specific needs of newcomers, which are very different from those of *long-term ELs (LTELs)* or *never-identified ELs (NIELs)*. In this book, I will use *MLs* to emphasize the wide range of English proficiencies implied by these terms, and *newcomers* to emphasize recent arrivals to the country. *Dually identified* students who need special education and English-as-a-second-language support are sometimes known as *SPED-ESLs*, in addition to *ELs/SPED*, *SPEDELs*, or *MLs/SPED*. Some MLs have also been dually identified as gifted MLs *(GMLs)*. Students who are in *bilingual* or *dual-language immersion* programs are known as *DL students*.

MYTH

All MLs can be in the same ESL classroom.

Newcomers

Newcomers are recent arrivals, and they might also be *students with interrupted formal education (SIFEs)* if their education was interrupted in their native country or they were never able to attend school. They will exhibit low levels of language and literacy in their home language. Newcomers may have come to the United States as unaccompanied minors and perhaps are now experiencing homesickness or homelessness. Newcomers might be labeled in schools as *immigrants*, *refugees*, *undocumented migrants*, or *recently arrived English learners (RAELs)*. Other newcomers might come *highly educated (HE)* because they received formal schooling in their native country. They probably studied English in their native country and developed strong language and literacy skills. Often, they are better in mathematics and geography than non-MLs. For these newcomers, it will be easier to fit and thrive in their U.S. schools.

Many MLs in the upper grades have more than likely learned to read in their home language. Some MLs might have even been exposed to reading in English. Nevertheless, their reading progress is wholly dependent on their English language development (ELD).

Long-Term English Learners

Of California's more than 6 million public school students, 1.148 million are MLs, and 200,000 of these students in Grades 6–12 are LTELs. What is so devastating about LTELs is that many of them were born in the United States and might be second- or third-generation residents/citizens of this country. They are MLs who have been in U.S. schools for six or more years without reaching levels of English proficiency to be reclassified (Olsen, 2014). This is truly an injustice!

Another 130,000 MLs are considered at risk of becoming LTELs unless teachers are better prepared to teach them. The proportion of MLs in Grades 6–12 in California who are LTELs ranges from 12 percent to 83 percent among districts with at least 25 LTEL students (Olsen, 2014).

The students come from one of nine language backgrounds, but the majority speak Spanish (Buenrostro & Maxwell-Jolly, 2021). In New York City, students come from many more language backgrounds. In Texas, the number of LTELs is about 20 percent of the total student population, or about 1.1 million. LTELs and all MLs are running out of time to catch up from the loss of attendance in school since the COVID-19 shutdown. They will need to accelerate their language, literacy, and content learning (Cashiola & Potter, 2020).

Several studies highlight experiences that LTELs share due to the lack of quality instruction in elementary schools (National Academies of Sciences, Engineering, and Medicine, 2017; Olsen, 2010, 2014):

- Variability of instructional approaches

- Lack of appropriate language development

- Teachers who lack preparation to integrate language, literacy, and content instruction

- Undiagnosed or unaddressed learning disability

To these, we (Calderón & Minaya-Rowe, 2011; Calderón & Montenegro, 2021) would add that their previous instruction was lacking:

- ✓ Academic language development

- ✓ Appropriate reading foundations or no reading instruction in prior years

- ✓ Explicit instruction of vocabulary, grammatical features, and sentence structures
- ✓ Sufficient or no explicit development of social-emotional competencies
- ✓ Ample opportunities for interaction with peers to practice discourse
- ✓ Consistent instructional language and literacy routines across the content areas

Teaching reading has been a challenge for most teachers in the past twenty or so years. Overall, the lack of preparation in language and literacy has limited LTELs' learning in the core subjects. Popular curriculum materials and limited professional development offerings have done little to help teachers move away from that trend.

Not Counted as English Learners

Immigrant students coming by the thousands daily are not yet included, as noted earlier, in the 5.3 million count (NCES, 2024). Neither are those who exited English learner (EXEL) status by passing the required assessments. They are no longer labeled as ELs even though monitoring and necessary services must continue for two years.

Also, parents have the prerogative to opt out of EL services, often doing so because they believe their children will not learn English fast enough. Heritage students are bilingual students who are achieving at grade level, which means the school does not have to administer a language assessment or label the student as an EL.

Making up part of the unidentified group are the thousands of immigrant students arriving daily. Schools will likely need time to identify them. Some may be unaccompanied minors or unhoused children who will be moving around the city or country for some time before they can be officially identified for special services.

Recommended Services for Multilingual Learners

Upon arrival at a school, MLs are assessed to determine their English-speaking, listening, reading, and writing proficiencies. Most state departments of education use six levels (see Figure 2.2). However, a coach works with a teacher to collect qualitative data from student or family interviews, student surveys, or conversations with students.

Figure 2.2   Proficiency Levels

EXAMPLES OF LEVELS OF ENGLISH PROFICIENCY

ASSESSMENT	LEVEL 1	LEVEL 2	LEVEL 3	LEVEL 4	LEVEL 5	LEVEL 6
WIDA Consortium: ACCESS	Beginning	Emerging	Developing	Expanding	Bridging	Reaching
English Language Proficiency Assessment for California (ELPAS)	Emerging		Expanding		Bridging	
Texas English Language Proficiency Assessment System (TELPAS)	Beginning	Intermediate	Advanced	High Advanced		
New York State English as a Second Language Achievement Test (NYSESLAT)	Entering	Emerging	Transitioning	Expanding	Commanding	

WIDA ACCESS, one of the broadly used assessments for MLs, uses the six levels as guidelines for how MLs engage with curriculum and how educators can work together to address their needs (WIDA, 2020). The WIDA website (https://wida.wisc.edu/) has many tools that can help teachers and coaches learn more about the instruction of MLs and MLs' needs at different proficiency levels.

Regardless of the diverse levels of English proficiency and literacy backgrounds, teachers of MLs need the following skills and dispositions to provide services required by the U.S. Department of Justice Civil Rights Division and U.S. Department of Education Office for Civil Rights (2015, 2023), which offer these guidelines for providing specific extended time during the day, after school, or in summer school:

▶ Level 1 and 2 MLs and newcomers at any point throughout the year must have additional ELD instruction by a certified ESL specialist and well-prepared teachers the remainder of the day.

▶ Level 3 and 4 MLs and SIFEs or LTELs might only have thirty to sixty minutes a week from ESL/ELD teachers and will have to rely mostly on specialized quality instruction from all their teachers who most likely need to be trained/retrained and coached.

▶ Level 5 MLs and EXELs will need the instruction that will sustain their growth and academic success; thus, their teachers will need training/retraining and coaching on providing rigorous but relevant and mindful instruction.

▶ Dually identified students will need highly qualified ESL/ELD and special education co-teachers who will need training/ retraining and coaching.

Support in Core Content Classrooms

▶ Allow MLs to demonstrate their knowledge and talents through multimodalities (music, movement, technology, projects, drama, etc.), not just traditional tests.

▶ Recognize and value the students' background and talents in their home language and culture. Use that knowledge to build upon it.

▶ Caveat. Due to the diversity of MLs, one cannot place all newcomers in one class and all LTELs in another or, worse yet, both groups together in one class! Some LTELs will do very well in verbal discourse but need for their teachers to focus on reading comprehension skills whereas some schooled newcomers will do very well in writing but need help and practice in speaking and listening. All students need targeted instruction specific to their needs (see Figure 2.3).

▶ Teachers and administrators must provide coaches with specific information about the MLs in the classroom they are about to observe and collect information for feedback to the teacher.

Coaches Can Help Schools Adhere to Federal Regulations

In a recent resource for families and educators titled *Protecting Access to Education for Migratory Children*, the U.S. Department of Justice Civil Rights Division and U.S. Department of Education Office for Civil Rights (2023) issued the following:

1. K–12 public schools must be open to all students, including migratory children, regardless of their or their parents' immigration status. Additionally, Title VI of the Civil Rights Act of 1964 prohibits public schools from discriminating based on race, color, or national origin.

2. Public schools must offer language assistance services to K–12 students who have limited English proficiency, including migratory children. Schools must identify these students as ELs so that they can receive services to enable them to meaningfully participate in the school's educational programs.

3. Public schools must make information about enrollment, classes, and other educational programs and activities accessible to parents and guardians who have limited English proficiency. Schools can accomplish this by providing accurate written translation or oral interpretation.

4. Students dually identified as ELs and in need of special education (sometimes called SPED-ESLs, ELs/SPED, MLs/SPED, or SPEDELs) must receive services from both programs.

5. Concerning GMLs, discrimination is also prohibited based on color, race, or national origin from participating in programs such as Advanced Placement (AP), International Baccalaureate (IB), dual enrollment in colleges, or any activity that receives federal funds. This way, MLs can meaningfully participate in all educational programs and services at the school.

Figure 2.3   Services by Proficiency Level

Due to their diverse levels of English proficiency and literacy backgrounds, MLs need the following services:

Newcomers & Level 1 & 2 Students	Level 3 & 4 Students	Level 5 & Recently Exited Students	Dually Identified Students
English development instruction by a certified ESL specialist	30 to 60 minutes a week from an ESL/ELD teacher	Instruction that will sustain their growth and academic success	Highly qualified ESL/ELD and special education co-teachers

MLs also need well-prepared teachers and coaches who can provide rigorous but relevant and mindful instruction throughout the day!

Source: Graphic by Leticia M. Trower

Equity, Inclusion, and Diversity Considerations

The coach can spearhead discussions on equity and diversity in staff meetings or professional learning communities (PLCs).

- Age appropriateness and grade level
- Disability and abilities
- Ethnicity, nationality, and race
- Family structure
- Gender equity and sexual orientation
- Health, safety, and environment
- Local/cultural norms and gestures
- Mental health
- Religion, morality, and politics
- Socioeconomic status

Common Questions From the Field About Multilingual Learners

✓ How do we learn about the diversity of our students' multilingual background experiences, knowledge, talents, aspirations, language, and literacy, and how do we serve our MLs well? Here is an example.

Vignette: Marilu González

Marilu González has been in this country for two years. She arrived from southern Mexico at the age of 11 speaking some Spanish but mostly Nahuatl. She is now in the seventh grade and has moved from a Level 1 proficiency in English to a Level 3 in speaking (see Figure 2.4). Her oral fluency is progressing in this grade because she wants to graduate from middle school with her friends. Her greatest challenge is reading comprehension now that she must read social studies texts and short novels instead of stories. Her ESL and English language arts (ELA) teacher have reached out to the ML coach for help.

(Continued)

(Continued)

> *The ML coach suggests that they have a planning meeting and invite the social studies and mathematics teachers so that they can all plan together. The first thing they do is to request assessment, placement, and any other information from the district office. They use a graphic organizer to display the information, not only for Marilu but for three other students who are striving at this grade level. The interdisciplinary team will also seek opportunities to speak to the students directly to learn more about them and their preferences, talents, and plans.*

Figure 2.4   Background Knowledge About Our Multilingual Learners

NAME	ENGLISH LANGUAGE PROFICIENCY LEVEL	PRIMARY LANGUAGE BACKGROUND	BACKGROUND INFORMATION	CLASSROOM(S) PLACEMENT	SCHEDULE
Marilu González	ACCESS Level 3	Low literacy levels in Spanish and oral fluency in Nahuatl	Arrived from southern Mexico two years ago. Needs reading development. Loves fashion magazines.	ELA: Ms. Schmidt ESL: Ms. Ortega Prealgebra: Mr. Lee Social Studies: Ms. Brown	8:30 a.m. 9:30 a.m. 11:00 a.m. 1:00 p.m.

online resources   Available for download at http://resources.corwin.com/CMLExcellence

✓   How do we convince our colleagues to stop teaching today's MLs the same way we did twenty-five years ago?

Go gently into that good night. Signaling out reluctant teachers might be counterproductive. Instead, ask the leadership to provide brief professional development or refreshers for everyone at the school on one of the most current instructional strategies. Attend these sessions with the reluctant teachers and show them how you can support them. Together, come up with a plan and a schedule before you leave the professional learning session.

✓   How do we adjust our coaching tools and competencies?

Observation tools for vocabulary, reading, and writing are provided in the next chapters, along with rationale and descriptions of these instructional practices. You and the teacher can plan where you want to begin.

✓   There are already too many competing professional development initiatives. How can we prevent teacher burnout?

Use your leadership and influence to help put together a team that can look at all the initiatives and examine how they overlap, how they conflict and contradict each other, and how they have not worked for MLs over all these years; otherwise, they would be achieving academically. Next, begin to see where changes can be made, some gradually, some immediately.

✓   The controversy about the Science of Reading for MLs is blocking progress. How can we address that?

We have known for almost twenty years about what works for MLs in the upper grades when it comes to literacy development alongside language and content learning as described in the research and practice chapters in this book and other publications (August & Shanahan, 2006, 2008; Calderón, 2007; Calderón & Tartaglia, 2023). We also know what doesn't work: too much focus on phonics, especially in the upper grades, where there is no evidence that overwhelming students with phonics helps striving readers (Shanahan, 2024a).

What Coaches Do to Highlight Multilingual Learners' Program Needs

Coaches can highlight other factors that have contributed to the lack of success of so many MLs in so many schools/school districts. When you see only instructional assistants and ESL/ELD teachers working with MLs, bring up the fact that MLs need to spend their whole schooling day with well-prepared core content teachers who know how to scaffold and adjust their teaching to reach them. You can also point out what else there is a need for:

▶   Comprehensive evidence-based curricula and instructional practices for MLs

▶   Additional comprehensive evidence-based professional development or coaching for some teachers

▶   Administrators' support to break the cycle of neglect and underachievement of certain MLs

▶   Appropriate allocation of funds for curricula

▶   More knowledge about the diversity of MLs in the school

What Coaches Do to Identify Multilingual Learners

Multilingual students come from a variety of economic, linguistic, cultural, religious, and ethnic backgrounds and experiences. Some newcomers have limited formal education and may have spent a portion of their lives in refugee camps. Others may be unhoused and experiencing different levels of posttraumatic stress disorder (PTSD). Depending on their backgrounds, different students hold significantly different expectations about how to initiate and sustain conversations, how to interact with teachers and peers, how to identify and solve different types of problems, and how to accomplish particular reading and writing tasks (Delpit, 1995). Therefore, teachers will need to make explicit the tacit reasoning processes, strategies, and discourse protocols that successful students know how to use. They will also need to provide a lot of understanding and love.

As a multilingual multiliteracy coach, you can help teachers use the charts at the end of this chapter (Figures 2.5–2.11) to identify students in the classes they teach throughout the day and begin to learn more about them.

Multilingual Learners' Levels of English Proficiency and Teacher/Coach Efficacy

The U.S. Department of Justice Civil Rights Division and U.S. Department of Education Office for Civil Rights (2023) require schools to do all of the following:

1. Have meaningful access to grade-level content with state education agencies monitoring local schools and districts to make sure this occurs.

2. Implement evidence-based instruction and technology with MLs.

3. Show student progress in learning English.

4. Engage in programming that includes English proficiency benchmarks to ensure that MLs are showing progress in learning English and the steps to be taken if they aren't.

5. Monitor MLs for two years after they demonstrate the capacity to do ordinary work in English and provide remedies when needed.

What Coaches Do: Take a Closer Look

Ask the teachers you coach to give you a seating chart indicating where MLs are sitting:

    a. Just arrived migrants/immigrants

    b. Newcomers who have been in the school one to two years

    c. MLs or LTELs who have been in U.S. schools for six or more years

    d. Reclassified (R) MLs who still need support for two years after reclassification

    e. Unaccompanied minors who will need extra care and social-emotional support

What We Must Keep in Mind

The Carnegie panel on adolescent literacy (Short & Fitzsimmons, 2007) established that MLs need to do twice the learning and twice the work because they are learning English at the same time as mathematics, science, social studies, language arts, physical education, career and technical arts, and electives—and they only have four years or fewer to graduate from high school. After-school tutoring or specialized summer school will help accelerate their learning (Short & Fitzsimmons, 2007). Coaching their teachers will make double the impact on their literacy development and core subjects learning (Calderón, 1984, 2007; Soto et al., 2024).

MLs Do Double the Work Because They Must Learn . . .

▶ Academic language for each subject area

▶ To read different types of texts

▶ To use a specific writing genre for each subject

▶ To prepare to graduate from high school in a timely manner

▶ To function within the classroom cultures of diverse teachers

▶ To develop peer relationships in a new culture and language

Myths That Have Held MLs Back

For years educators have been saying that it takes five to seven years for a child to exit ESL services. This is true in schools where little quality attention is paid to MLs and only the ESL or one bilingual teacher is responsible for their learning English. In schools where all content teachers attend the same professional development sessions together and participate in coaching, students can exit from EL status in two or three years and graduate on time. When these features are in place—teacher efficacy, school structures such as course access, integrated classrooms, heterogeneous group work, co-teaching, and administrator support—MLs break the myth that it takes five to seven years (Abreu, 2011; Calderón, 2007).

MYTH

It takes five to seven years to learn English.

Programs and Instructional Structures for Multilingual Learners in Secondary Schools

English as a second language and English language development are the main programs where an ESL/ELD teacher either pulls students out of classes for ESL instruction, goes into core content classrooms to work with small groups of teachers, or teaches a self-contained group. Schools in some states also offer sheltered mathematics, science, or other subjects taught by a second-language specialist. Some middle and high schools throughout the country are beginning to offer dual-language programs and courses. These are taught in two languages (e.g., Spanish and English, Chinese and English, or Haitian Creole and English). While there are different models for dual-language instruction, devoting 50 percent of the coursework to each language is the ideal goal. Most notably, the goal of dual-language instruction is to promote language and literacy development in two languages. There is a significant research base supporting the many cognitive, academic, and social benefits of multilingualism (Calderón & Carreón, 1994; National Academies of Sciences, Engineering, and Medicine, 2017).

Course Access

One important factor that influences high school graduation and postsecondary readiness is course access. All MLs need to have access to rigorous instruction and AP courses. In many cases, MLs are placed in tracks where access to advanced instruction is nil. While ESL and sheltered classes in high school help MLs develop language and literacy, particularly for newcomers, the irony is that if they are kept for too many semesters in those courses, it will take time away from courses that help develop academic content language, knowledge, and requirements necessary for timely graduation. MLs' learning progress must be monitored, as well as the classroom context. Low-level instruction in any classroom will inevitably lower MLs' engagement because students get bored when they feel unchallenged. Lack of rigor and interest might even lead to dropping out of school.

MYTH

You should shelter MLs from rigorous courses.

Segregated Courses

Another drawback when students are segregated into ESL/ELD or sheltered courses is that they don't have an opportunity to develop relationships with students who are not MLs. Even in classrooms with non-MLs, it is important to group MLs in heterogeneous teams (e.g., MLs and non-MLs with different genders, ethnicities, and languages). It benefits all students because this is where social skills, tolerance, empathy, and understanding of other cultures are fomented for all students in the class. Chapter 3, on reading, shares ideas for how and when to group students to make sure that MLs are not clustered by proficiency levels. They need to be in heterogeneous teams with English-speaking role models. Although LTELs may appear to be quite fluent in English, they still will benefit from exposure to students with higher levels of academic English to increase their academic reading and writing skills.

MYTH

Do not teach newcomers to read until they speak English.

Discourse for Reading Comprehension

We want to hear MLs, especially newcomers, start talking in classes from day one. Therefore, text-based talk is necessary from the start. Teachers can begin by making sure that MLs learn instructional words that are used every day, such as "follow directions," "deduce," "it's the paragraph at the top of the page," "scroll to the bottom of page 4," "highlight the main ideas only," and "use the steps in your guide." Students can practice summarizing for peers after a teacher's explanation or after they read each paragraph with a partner by using a variety of sentence starters from a simple "I think this says" or "Can you clarify this for me?" to a more complex "My inference here is . . ." The chapters on reading (Chapter 3) and vocabulary (Chapter 4) provide examples.

MYTH

The ESL teacher should work with MLs in the back of the classroom.

Co-Teaching

Chapter 1 touched upon the benefits of collaboration between ESL/ELD teachers and content teachers. When these two types of teachers have the opportunity to share their expertise and co-teach, the benefits to MLs are significantly enhanced. A qualified ESL teacher understands the specific language demands of a unit or lesson while the content teacher brings not only a deep knowledge of content but also an understanding of how to teach and assess the content. When the content teacher participates in the language-literacy-content professional development, both teachers can teach a lesson on vocabulary and reading comprehension embedded in the content instructional process. Co-teaching, when thoughtfully implemented, can result in great gains in both ELD and content mastery. Moreover, it can be a vehicle for giving ESL and content course credit to MLs in one class.

With that said, a common obstacle to co-teaching is the ESL teacher's availability. For effective schoolwide implementation, an ESL teacher would need to partner with every content teacher who is responsible for educating MLs. However, this doesn't mean that administrators shouldn't work to support co-teaching configurations whenever possible. Keep in mind that administrators are also responsible for master scheduling, which can open opportunities for co-teaching. Moreover, effective co-teaching usually depends on additional training—often at an additional cost—which is all the more reason that school leaders must be fully committed to the mission of excellent instruction for MLs.

When co-teaching is possible, a coach might provide valuable support in orchestrating co-planning and recommending specific co-teaching configurations and practices. Even in the absence of a coach, both teachers can become peer coaches for one another and benefit from the additional pair of eyes. A special workshop or collegial opportunity to study books on co-teaching such as Honigsfeld et al.'s *From Equity Insights to Action* (2022) can refine their practice.

While co-teaching between two bilingual teachers (for instance an English and a Spanish teacher) is rare at the secondary level, this configuration would be beneficial for students. Without discounting the multiple benefits of supporting the sustainability of students' home languages, educators and researchers agree that to succeed in school and participate in civic life in the United States, all children must develop strong English proficiency and literacy skills (Olsen, 2014; Slavin & Calderón, 2001). Bear in mind that cultural and linguistic sustainability and English language proficiency are not mutually exclusive—despite the beliefs of some policymakers. In fact, many educators and researchers support the acquisition of English and the primary language to help deepen English skills and continue to develop the primary language. The social and cultural benefits of developing proficiency in the primary language are beneficial to the student, their home community, and the business sector (National Academies of Sciences, Engineering, and Medicine, 2017).

Benefits We Find for Co-Teaching by ESL and Core Content Teachers

▶ The content teacher gets instructional support for the MLs.

▶ The ESL teacher has an opportunity to model and even coach the content teacher.

▶ The content teacher gets a personal coach by working with the ESL teacher.

▶ The ESL teacher learns more profoundly about a topic.

▶ All students benefit from this partnership.

Caveat. There may not be sufficient ESL teachers in the school or district to team up with all the core content teachers who have MLs. There is one possible solution. ESL teachers work with the same subject-area teachers for a while. For example, an ESL teacher works with an Algebra 1 teacher for six weeks or one semester, then does the same with an Algebra 2 or geometry teacher. Another ESL teacher can work with science or social studies teachers. During those weeks with the ESL teacher, the content teacher will be practicing new strategies with support from the ESL teacher and the coach. The triad will contribute to the continuation of quality implementation of the strategies for teaching MLs learned at the schoolwide professional development.

Administrators' Messaging and Support Structures

Feedback and support for teachers by administrators need to emphasize rigorous but supportive instruction for MLs. Deficit views of MLs' potential can impact the amount and quality of their coursework. Coaches can help school leaders and teachers make content accessible with explicit vocabulary and reading instructional practices. Language and literacy support integrated into content lessons is a coach's main task. Concomitantly, a coach can advocate for MLs by looking for ways to strengthen teachers' belief in MLs' potential.

Coach's main task: Support integration of language and literacy into all subjects.

Coach's concomitant task: Help teachers believe more in MLs' potential.

As stated previously, there are many ways in which administrators can support co-teaching such as in the development of master schedules. Whether the schedule allows for co-planning or not, supplying time and space for ESL teachers to participate in common planning time carries its benefits. When observing a co-teaching situation, discuss the delivery plan beforehand.

Coaches can prepare to notice and inform the teachers, "Does the language of instruction dovetail with the content instruction?" There is more to observing the configurations and orchestrations of co-teaching and coaching in the following chapters.

So Far, the Best Approach Is Language and Literacy Across the Curriculum

The best way for MLs to accelerate language and academic learning is for coaches to prepare, retool, and support all mathematics, science, social studies, technology, engineering, arts, physical education, music, career education, and electives teachers on how to infuse vocabulary, reading comprehension, content-based writing, and social-emotional competencies into their core content areas. When the use of cooperative learning undergirds the integrated instructional approach, it also addresses and develops the social-emotional competencies that benefit all students and helps to identify potential problems. You will see how students work in pairs, triads, and quads to practice and develop speaking, listening, reading, writing, and social skills in the following chapters.

Building on MLs' Academic, Experiential, and Cultural Background Knowledge

Teachers can draw on the students' academic, experiential, and cultural knowledge to accelerate their learning. Here are some things to consider.

Students in each category of MLs come to school with a home language. Although their typical academic knowledge will vary from the "traditional knowledge" culture in the United States, some may know more about mathematics, geography, and world literature than general education students. Their literacy practices might not match those we use, but those can be built upon (Sugarman, 2023).

To this I would add that when we know their histories, we discover their strengths. Help the teachers shape the positive identities of MLs by embracing their linguistic and cultural diversity. Besides academic knowledge, MLs have experiences, talents, and specific knowledge derived from sports, music, farming, cooking, water conservation, storytelling, and work experience at various jobs. Many know how to use technology, at least a phone, but many others do not. Some are great artists and can use that talent to display their learning through drawing, movement, and construction of projects.

Messages From the National Academies of Sciences, Engineering, and Medicine

The National Academies of Sciences, Engineering, and Medicine (2017) panel points to promising practices for ML instruction in middle and high schools that coaches can help promote.

Education of MLs in Middle Schools

1. The student's primary language must be used, when possible, to develop academic English in specific content areas.

2. Teachers should use collaborative, peer-group learning communities to support and extend teacher-led instruction.

3. Texts and other instructional materials should be at the same grade level as those used by English-proficient peers.

Education of MLs in High Schools

1. Develop academic English and its varied grammatical structures and vocabulary intensively as part of subject-matter learning.

2. Integrate oral and written language instruction into content-area teaching.

3. Provide regular structured opportunities to develop written language skills.

4. Develop the reading and writing abilities of MLs through text-based, analytical instruction using cognitive strategies.

5. Provide direct and explicit comprehension strategy instruction.

6. Provide opportunities for extended discussion of text meaning and interpretation.

7. Foster student motivation and engagement in literacy learning.

8. Provide regular peer-assisted learning opportunities.

9. Provide small-group instructional opportunities to students struggling in areas of literacy and ELD.

What Coaches Do to Support a Positive School Climate for Multilingual Learners

A coach can help create a safe and respectful school climate where MLs feel valued and comfortable speaking and learning. Here are some ways a coach can help:

- Consider reviewing the school's strengths-based policies and practices that might be restricting effective relevant coaching and teaching practices.

- Propose assets-based, instead of deficit, mindsets and practices for engaging students and their families.

- Student health is a large part of learning. Help ensure that all students and their families have access to affordable health care by suggesting to all stakeholders that all low-income unaccompanied children be eligible for public health insurance or social-emotional programs as soon as they leave Office of Refugee Resettlement custody.

What Coaches Do for the Classroom's Positive Climate

- Use different observational criteria for GMLs and dually identified MLs/SPED that is developed jointly with teachers, counselors, and site administrators.

- Help the school's committee on gifted students remove any barriers impinging on GMLs' progress.

- Help others learn about the newly arrived immigrant students— their recent struggles and most pressing needs.

- Provide feedback to the teacher and help decide where to further assist these courageous students.

- Help teachers identify social-emotional competencies that might become problems.

- Continue to improve vision, motivation, knowledge, practice, and reflection for all teachers.

- Meet with other coaches, whether in person or online, in the same district or by reaching out to other coaching communities, to exchange ideas, solve problems, and celebrate successes.

- Share the charts in Figures 2.5–2.11 with teachers and school leaders so they can get more precise and practical information about their MLs and the qualified staff or needed staff.

First, ML coaches might want to use this checklist for in-depth discussions (Figure 2.5).

Figure 2.5 Checklist for Collaborative Discussions

Who Are Our MLs?

- ☐ What are our students' proficiency levels for listening, speaking, reading, and writing?
- ☐ How many are LTELs?
- ☐ How many are SIFEs?
- ☐ How many are newcomers?
- ☐ How many are refugees?
- ☐ How many are/who might be gifted and talented?
- ☐ Who might need special education support?
- ☐ What background knowledge do they already have about a subject?
- ☐ What do we know about their life experiences (trauma/no trauma, home situation, special skills, and knowledge they developed during this educational hiatus)?
- ☐ What are their talents?
- ☐ What are their interests?
- ☐ MLs come with great knowledge and rich experiences; how can we discover them?

 Available for download at http://resources.corwin.com/CMLExcellence

Figure 2.6 Number of Multilingual Learners and Personnel in Our School

Write the Number of Students Under Each Category

EMERGENT BILINGUALS	NEWCOMERS	SIFEs	DUALLY IDENTIFIED MLs/SPED	LONG-TERM ELs	GIFTED MLs	NOT IDENTIFIED AS MLs

 Available for download at http://resources.corwin.com/CMLExcellence

Figure 2.7 Language Proficiency Levels of Our Multilingual Learners

Write the Levels of English Proficiency for Each Category

EMERGENT BILINGUALS	NEWCOMERS	SIFEs	DUALLY IDENTIFIED MLs/SPED	LONG-TERM ELs	GIFTED MLs	NOT IDENTIFIED AS MLs

online resources Available for download at http://resources.corwin.com/CMLExcellence

Figure 2.8 Instructional Personnel in Our Middle School

GRADE LEVEL	ESL/ ELD	ELA	SOCIAL STUDIES	SCIENCE	MATHEMATICS	OTHER SUBJECTS
6						
7						
8						

online resources Available for download at http://resources.corwin.com/CMLExcellence

Figure 2.9 Instructional Personnel in Our High School

GRADE LEVEL	ESL/ ELD	ELA	SOCIAL STUDIES	SCIENCE	MATHEMATICS	OTHER SUBJECTS
9						
10						
11						
12						

online resources Available for download at http://resources.corwin.com/CMLExcellence

Figure 2.10   Names of Teachers in Our School

SUBJECT AREAS	ESL/ELD TEACHERS	GENERAL EDUCATION TEACHERS	TEACHER ASSISTANTS
Science			
Mathematics			
Social Studies			
ELA			
STEM or			
STEAM (science, technology, engineering, the arts, and mathematics)			
Music			
Physical Education			
Other			

online resources   Available for download at http://resources.corwin.com/CMLExcellence

Figure 2.11   Administrators/Leadership in Our School

PRINCIPAL	ASSISTANT PRINCIPALS	COORDINATORS	COACHES	OTHERS

online resources   Available for download at http://resources.corwin.com/CMLExcellence

Message From a Special Guest: Coaching Teachers of Multilingual Learners

By Mariana Castro

The effectiveness of instructional coaching as a way to support the professional development of teachers is supported by research (Archibald et al., 2011). One of the main reasons for its effectiveness is that it is job-embedded; that is, teachers receive it within the scope and context of their job, resulting in timely and highly relevant learning. Another reason is that instructional coaching typically focuses on both content and practice—not just one or the other. For someone teaching mathematics, they must know both the content of mathematics and the practice of teaching mathematics. For coaches of teachers who work with MLs, this becomes even more complex, since teachers must know about the subject matter, about language, and about how to teach both in an integrated manner. However, the complexity of this task is what makes coaching most effective. Through coaching, instructional coaches can serve as thought partners, guides, and support for the process of experimenting, reflecting, and improving these challenging practices.

Research has shown that effective teacher professional development and coaching can lead to significant improvements in teaching, including increased student achievement and teacher self-efficacy, which has the related benefit of job satisfaction and retention (Joyce & Showers, 1982b; Knight, 2022; National Research Council, 2010).

Here are some important considerations related to coaching teachers of MLs:

Time

Coaches work closely with educators over an extended period, providing targeted feedback, modeling effective instructional strategies, and collaborating on lesson planning. This means that coaches need time to plan, meet, and reflect with teachers and on their own about the work with those teachers. It is not enough to assign a coach; it is important to create structures and workloads that are fair to both teachers and coaches. Another implication is that coaching results take time because it takes time to change practice, experiment, and feel comfortable with new approaches. Coaching needs to be a consistent and long-term activity and not a one-time event.

Focus

The focus for the coaching needs to be co-constructed between the coach and the teacher, but there are four basic areas it should cover:

Cultural Competence

It is important for coaches to be familiar and share background on working with students from various cultures. Culture can be invisible to those whose cultural background matches that of the school whereas it can be a challenge for those whose cultural background differs from it. Because of the differential in power status between teachers and students, some of these differences can be misunderstood or ignored. Understanding cultural differences can help teachers connect with students and find ways to connect the content to their life experiences.

Linguistic Knowledge

While it may be impossible to know all of the languages students speak in a school, having a background in linguistic differences can be useful for educators. A coach with a sociolinguistics or Teachers of English to Speakers of Other Languages (TESOL) background has spent time learning about language differences and may point them out as well as have ideas or strategies to help develop metalinguistic skills not only for the teachers but also among students.

Language Development

Just as important as knowing the linguistics (content) behind languages, it is also relevant to understand how to help students develop language (practice). Whether students are being taught in one (English-only) or two (bilingual) languages, paying attention to language or bilingual development is key. Knowing how and when to introduce language within the teaching cycle and when to focus more on content is important to ensure students learn language in context without becoming overwhelmed.

Content Knowledge

At the end of the day, we want all students to be successful in learning the content (e.g., mathematics, science, language arts). It is important for coaches to provide examples and strategies to scaffold content so that all students have access and the opportunity to learn the same content as other students. Coaches can provide tools and strategies, but most importantly, they can share the knowledge and practice on when and how to use them appropriately, matching language abilities and learning styles.

All of these considerations are relevant during instruction and assessment. Knowing how to scaffold to ensure students are able to learn the content is just as important as scaffolding an assessment to ensure students are able to demonstrate what they have learned and are able to do. Thinking critically about objectives, activities to achieve those objectives, and valid ways to assess the learning are all opportunities for coaches to engage in collaborative thought partnership with teachers. Experimentation is also

(Continued)

(Continued)

important because what works for most students does not always work for MLs, and coaching should provide the safety and flexibility to try new approaches when the traditional ones fall short.

Lastly, no one has all the knowledge, and even if someone did, the field of education is constantly evolving and producing new research. Coaches need time and peers to make sense of new research and consider if and how to align new ideas to the mission and vision for the program. Investing in coaches is investing in our teachers and ultimately in the success of all our students.

Mariana Castro, PhD, is the qualitative research director at the Multilingual Learning Research Center, School of Education, University of Wisconsin. She also conducts workshops on effective ML instruction and coaching.

From One Coach to Another

What has made coaching easy for me is focusing on the teacher's agenda, not my own. ExC-ELL provides a framework and a variety of strategies, and the beauty of the coaching sessions is the opportunity they provide to not only give the teacher feedback on their implementation but also use years of experience with ExC-ELL in a variety of classroom contexts to provide ideas, insights, or suggestions for implementing the strategy or better engaging students. Listening to teachers' implementation needs and providing them with possible solutions to try in response to any challenges is a form of collaboration from which I believe both the coach and the teacher benefit. The teacher gets to hear an outside perspective and can consider things in ways they may not have before. The coach learns about ways ExC-ELL is being implemented and is able to provide support and guidance to help meet the teacher's needs. This focus on the teacher's objectives and the needs of the students, rather than an external agenda being opposed, helps to create a level of collaboration and trust that I believe helps teachers to grow as well as provides a space to create richer instructional experiences for students. I am grateful for the teachers who trust me to come into their classrooms, share what I see, and suggest ways to refine and enhance the great things that are already happening!

—Rebecca Upchurch, Instructional Coach, Loudoun County Public Schools; CEO and Clarity and Mindset Coach, Higher Good Coaching

Coaching Reading Teaching and Learning

CHAPTER #3

From One Coach to Another: Tips for Coaches of Teachers With Multilingual Learners

Coaching teachers with a focus on reading strategies is one of the most impactful ways to advance high-quality literacy instruction for our nation's multilingual learners. To see a teacher move from feeling unsure, to trying a new strategy bravely, to experiencing that aha moment remains a high-light of my career.

—Lillian Ardell, PhD, Founder of Language Matters, LLC

Where Are We in the International Reading Standing?

In reading, average scores for all students in the United States have declined to levels last seen in the 1970s for all students. The scores among the most disadvantaged students are even worse! Those in the bottom quarter of achievement are less proficient in reading than similar-aged peers were in 1971, posting the lowest scores ever recorded. Mathematics, which now requires more reading, has also seen a decline. Despite nearly $200 billion in emergency federal education spending, students have not progressed as was expected with all those resources (National Center for Education Statistics [NCES], 2023; Sawchuk, 2023).

Based on these disappointing data, many states and schools are now shifting toward Science of Reading (SoR) programs and materials. Some are selecting programs for multilingual learners (MLs) that have not been tested for evidence.

MYTHS ABOUT THE SCIENCE OF READING

- ▶ It is a program.
- ▶ One program fits all.
- ▶ It is only phonics.
- ▶ It is not for MLs.

The Reading League and National Committee for Effective Literacy (2023) have been working on clarifying these myths through a joint statement. Both sides of the initial debate now agree that the SoR is for MLs when the basic components identified by the National Literacy Panel for Language-Minority Children and Youth (August & Shanahan, 2006, 2008) are adequately enhanced to use in MLs' classrooms.

The joint statement emphasizes the importance of vocabulary and discourse for MLs as well as an assets-based approach to all aspects of literacy instruction. Above and beyond buying a program or materials, building capacity and skills among all teachers in the schools (since the population of MLs will continue to increase) is now the priority.

Regardless of the reading program selected, the teachers will need the expertise of an ML coach!

Regardless of the reading program selected, the teachers will need expert support from an ML coach. The NCES (2023) data illustrate that reading instruction needs to be revised and that this evidence-based approach can be a positive first step. The instructional model described in this chapter was tested for five years in middle and high schools with large populations of diverse MLs. In each case, the whole school adopted the model; hence the schools moved from low-performing to exemplary in two years (Abreu, 2011; Calderón & Minaya-Rowe, 2011; Calderón & Tartaglia, 2023). Each school had a different literacy program. Yet, each school prepared English language arts (ELA), English as a second language (ESL), and core content teachers to integrate the language and literacy strategies as described in each chapter.

Since reading in English is the strongest predictor of academic success (National Reading Panel, 2000), we recommend that reading continue to be taught explicitly whether an ML needs instruction in the early stages of foundations of reading—*phonemic and phonological awareness, decoding, vocabulary, fluency,* and *comprehension* (August & Shanahan, 2006, 2008)—or in the later stages—*multisyllabic words, affixes, fluency with automaticity, reading with prosody,* and *depth of comprehension* (Vaughn et al., 2022).

"Reading instruction must ensure that children have the opportunity to integrate learning the code (by developing skills in phonological awareness, letter knowledge, phoneme-grapheme relationships, spelling rules, and fluency) with learning all that is necessary to read for meaning (by developing skills in vocabulary, world knowledge, discourse structure, comprehension strategies, and purposes for reading)" (August & Shanahan, 2008, p. 29).

For older students, the primary focus of reading changes from "learning to read" to "reading to learn" (Chall, 1996). Research on reading clearly demonstrates that without mastery of decoding, there is no mastery of comprehension (Perfetti, 1985). This implies that the development of reading skills for MLs is definitely more challenging than for native speakers because MLs in the upper grades must do triple duty as they learn to speak in English, read in English, and read closely to master content. This will be especially challenging for students who do not have a reading foundation in their native language or a foundation in the cognitive and linguistic precursors to literacy.

August and Shanahan (2006, 2008) found from their meta-analyses that the development of reading comprehension, like that of word-level skills, is highly dependent on effective instruction. We surmount from those and more recent studies (Calderón & Montenegro, 2021; Calderón & Tartaglia, 2023; Zacarian et al., 2021) that ML coaches can help teachers meet the challenge of word knowledge and reading comprehension.

What Research Says About Teaching Reading to MLs

The National Reading Panel (2000) report identified five research-based elements necessary for providing successful literacy instruction: phonics, decoding, reading fluency, vocabulary, and reading comprehension.

(Continued)

(Continued)

Subsequently, the National Literacy Panel on Language-Minority Children and Youth compiled the research on the differences and similarities between language-minority and native speakers in the development of various literacy skills (primarily in elementary schools) in societal languages in addition to English (August & Shanahan, 2006).

Recently, the SoR debates brought back the importance of the "big five" (phonics, decoding, reading fluency, vocabulary, and comprehension). The Reading League and National Committee on Effective Literacy (2023) came out with a joint statement in an effort to integrate the "big five" with second-language premises and practices. The committee's specific recommendations on classroom application are still in progress. Reading in secondary schools has not been addressed as of the date of this publication.

Reading fluency reflects and is affected by language comprehension. Fluency has been called a bridge between word recognition and comprehension, as well as semantic and syntactic knowledge, accuracy of word reading, and automaticity of text reading with appropriate expression and prosody (Duke et al., 2021). To this, we add that explicit instruction on word recognition and word knowledge must precede reading a text to comprehend (Calderón, 2007). We call this preteaching of vocabulary, which is key for entering a text with some background and confidence. Preteaching of vocabulary ought to be taught in all elementary schools (d = 0.78) (Calderón et al., 1998) and at secondary schools (d = 0.92) in core content classrooms (Calderón, 2007; Calderón & Tartaglia, 2023).

The decision to put the reading chapter ahead of vocabulary does not preclude the importance of teaching vocabulary before students read. Reading comes first in this book because, currently, that is the one area in teaching MLs that needs the most attention.

Research on Reading in the Disciplines

The reading approach described in this chapter includes routines that build subject-area teaching and learning (e.g., oral language/discourse and vocabulary, as described in Chapter 4) and reading comprehension strategies, stamina, and schema.

- Strategies—routines that readers can use to support comprehension such as summarizing, inferencing, asking questions, and creating graphic organizers

▶ Stamina—the notion that students will gradually be able to read texts for sustained periods of time

▶ Schema—building knowledge by reading several texts on the same subject

The difference between MLs and non-MLs is that the oral language/discourse, vocabulary, and morphology need more time and more explicit instruction for MLs. The ML type of language-literacy teaching framework supports the following practices in the disciplines:

▶ Mathematical problem reading

▶ Working through scientific investigations

▶ Engineering problems and solutions

▶ Historical and literary argumentation

It helps students delve deeply into comprehension of a subject to become better readers of a variety of texts. The approach is grounded in scientific studies centered on MLs that panels of experts have gathered and on empirical studies commissioned by the Carnegie Corporation of New York (Calderón, 2007; Short & Fitzsimmons, 2007).

Both research on second-language literacy development (August & Shanahan, 2006; Gottlieb & Calderón, in press; Guilamo, 2022; National Academies of Sciences, Engineering, and Medicine, 2017) and emerging policy research (The Reading League & National Committee for Effective Literacy, 2023) clearly point to fundamental differences between monolingual children learning to read in their native languages and bilingual children learning to read in their second languages.

Due to the scarcity of dissemination of empirical studies on reading for MLs, schools are implementing some of the approaches that *are not evidence-based* or *have not been tested with secondary-level MLs*, and even use some programs that have a negative effect on MLs. Some examples of programs for which research panels found no positive effect sizes and that are still used with MLs are balanced literacy, reader's workshop, the whole-language approach, guided reading, the three-cueing system, and silent reading. We see these manifested in the appalling numbers of long-term English learners (LTELs) everywhere.

Scripted programs highly acclaimed and espoused by several state departments of education were not developed with MLs in their scope. The same is true for certain reading series or phonics-only materials or for programs that now carry the SoR label. The requirement to move quickly through a curriculum to stay on pace also leaves MLs behind. MLs need time to anchor language, literacy, and content.

"The National Center on Teacher Quality identified five key areas where education authorities can arm teachers with better skills to teach the fundamentals of literacy—from establishing strict training and licensure standards for trainees to funding meaningful professional development to classroom veterans" (Mahken, 2024). One of the key areas most relevant to this book is that twenty-one states don't establish any standards for the specific instruction of MLs.

A Report to the Carnegie Corporation of New York: "Double the Work"

In 2007, I was part of a team of researchers who were convened by the Carnegie Corporation of New York to generate recommendations based on existing studies of adolescent MLs' challenges and solutions to acquiring language and academic literacy. After two years of combing through the literature, the panel concluded that

> English language learners are still developing their proficiency in academic English at the same time they are studying core content areas through English. Thus, they must perform double the work of native English speakers in the country's middle and high schools. (Short & Fitzsimmons, 2007, p. 1 [see Executive Summary])

Since that report, we have learned that reading is the basis of academic English and that it needs more emphasis. The findings from 2007 still apply today and are restated in more recent panel reports such as *Guiding Principles for Dual Language Education* (Howard et al., 2018) and the synthesis of research from the National Academies of Sciences, Engineering, and Medicine (2017) titled *Promoting the Educational Success of Children and Youth Learning English: Promising Futures*.

Recommendations From the Carnegie Panel on Adolescent Literacy for Multilingual Learners

1. Integrate all four language skills (speaking, listening, reading, and writing) into instruction from the start.

2. Teach the components and processes for reading and writing.

3. Teach reading comprehension strategies.

4. Focus on developing vocabulary before, during, and after reading.

5. Build and activate background knowledge.

6. Teach language through content and themes.

7. Use native language strategically.

8. Pair technology with existing interventions.

9. Motivate MLs through choice.

Recent Studies on Comprehension

According to Shanahan (2023b), many studies confirm that teaching comprehension strategies can improve reading comprehension. He finds that too many readers (meaning non-MLs) are satisfied with comprehending a text in a superficial way. They don't retain enough information to be able to discuss the content. Strategies arm readers with purposeful actions they can take before, during, and after reading. Basically, they get readers to think about the ideas more than once. The idea of strategies is to provide readers with the tools that will allow them to accomplish purposeful learning—and the tools work by slowing readers down and getting them to think more than once about the ideas in the text.

MYTH

There are no scientific studies on secondary-level MLs.

Concerning reading for MLs, although we've had the Carnegie panel's publication (Short & Fitzsimmons, 2007) for almost two decades, we still don't see the recommendations being implemented. When my colleagues and I began observing in classrooms about twenty years ago, and as recently as a month ago, we noticed two prevalent reading approaches that did not work at all for MLs in secondary schools: independent silent reading (without teacher facilitation) or individually reading aloud when called to read in class. We followed students for three years and compared this type of classroom reading with the experimental ExC-ELL language-literacy reading approach. We discovered that the control group had not progressed in their language and reading skills as much as the ExC-ELL experimental group that was embedded in the reading sequence outlined in these chapters.

ExC-ELL Comprehension Strategies for MLs Are . . .

1. Grounded in constant vocabulary learning and discourse that uses new vocabulary

2. Explicit instruction of selected words/phrases from the text before students read (see Chapter 4 on which words to select)

3. Partner reading by alternating sentences

4. Verbally summarizing after each paragraph using words pretaught and new words learned from the paragraph

5. After-reading activities to consolidate language, literacy, and content learning

Multilingual Learners Are Not Reading Enough!

MLs are not reading for fun, nor are they reading textbooks or texts in their daily subject areas (but neither are most other students). Here are some reasons why some approaches have not worked for MLs (Calderón, 2020).

Reading Approaches That Do *Not* Work for MLs

1. Calling out students one by one to read aloud in class, or "popcorn reading" without rehearsal, is most embarrassing for students who mispronounce words, struggle with fluency, and cannot pay attention to what they are reading because of the stress. Not surprisingly, they are not able to tell us what they read. This is probably the reason why many LTELs became too embarrassed to read and hate reading.

2. Silent reading does not work for MLs without prior teacher introduction and partner reading. There are too many unknowns: (a) They might be not actually reading, just pretending to read. (b) They might be reading, but not understanding. (c) They are not able to assess or clarify their thinking with others; thus their ideas remain shallow. (d) They quickly forget what they read without verbal interaction; hence the language of the subject and the knowledge of the subject remain limited.

Source: **Calderón (2020).**

Digital Reading Materials

Other findings by Shanahan (2023a) have implications for MLs' reading. He found that digital books are read with lower comprehension and more mind wandering. Even more discouraging is that the more time students spend reading digitally in school, the lower their reading comprehension tends to be (Salmerón et al., 2023). This is something to consider if MLs are mainly relegated to online reading programs.

MYTH

If they don't understand during class instruction, MLs can read about the topic online.

Many studies have compared digital and traditional reading. Few studies, however, have explored the advantages of digital reading—and none are aimed at identifying strategies readers can use to adjust their digital reading in ways that will allow it to be successful. Likewise, as helpful as dictionary assistance is (it has been found to improve children's vocabulary), it isn't doing much either to improve comprehension or to help young readers achieve independence (Shanahan, 2023a). When we observe classrooms, we notice that these problems are exacerbated for MLs. They are offered dictionaries or translation devices to help their comprehension when reading a biology text. Would a dictionary help us read a text in German if we didn't know German that well? How long would it take us to comprehend the biology passage?

What Evidence-Based Reading Should Look Like in Middle and High School Classrooms With MLs

The way we can engage MLs with learning all that is necessary to read for meaning (by developing skills in vocabulary, world knowledge, discourse structure, comprehension strategies, and purposes for reading) is to use partner reading and summarization along with what happens before and after.

ExC-ELL Reading Comprehension in Middle and High Schools

Stage 1—Before Reading: Teach What They Will Need to Understand the Text

▶ Build students' background with historical facts and foundational information, even what we might think is common knowledge about a topic, and teach new words used in the reading segment (5 minutes).

▶ Build word knowledge by preteaching five keywords that will help make sense of the text they are about to read (10 minutes). (See Chapter 4 for information on preteaching vocabulary.)

(Continued)

(Continued)

▶ State the reason for reading, objectives, and norms of interaction between partners (3 minutes).

▶ Target reading skills. Teach students to monitor their comprehension as they read by modeling how to do all of the following:

  • Summarize together after each paragraph (2 minutes).

  • Use text features (pictures, captions, graphics, bullets, color) to get the gist of the text (2 minutes).

  • Identify text structure (cause and effect, problem and solution) (3 minutes).

  • Highlight language structures, such as by deconstructing a complex sentence (1 minute).

Caveat: Once students know how to summarize, all these steps do not have to be done in every lesson or every time students read.

Stage 2—During Reading: Use Partner Reading and Summarization to Help MLs Get the Most Out of Reading

▶ Pairs have been preselected and are sitting together ready to read.

▶ Pairs conduct partner reading, where partners read aloud alternating sentences (10 minutes).

▶ After reading a paragraph, partners stop and verbally summarize (or retell) what they read (5 minutes).

▶ The teacher leads the discussion on the section they read (5 minutes).

▶ Students ask and answer questions to better understand the text they read (5 minutes).

▶ Another 10-minute partner reading and summarization cycle is conducted with subsequent sections.

Stage 3—After Reading: Consolidation of Language, Literacy, and Content Knowledge

▶ The teacher conducts depth-of-word learning and sentence deconstruction/construction using samples from the text (5 minutes).

▶ Students go back to the text to do close reading or read additional texts on the subject and solidify the use of new vocabulary, reading comprehension and metacognitive skills, and content information (in 20 to 30 minutes) by doing one of the following:

  - Write Bloom-type questions (at knowledge, understanding, application, synthesis, evaluation, or creativity levels; see Armstrong, 2010) in teams instead of only answering book or worksheet questions.

  - Use a cooperative-competitive activity (see the Vignette: After Reading on page 91 for a description of this strategy) or other cooperative learning activities to consolidate learning of language, literacy, and content.

  - Map important facts in cognitive or graphic organizers.

  - Use teams of four for follow-up with reciprocal-reading-type roles (such as reader, summarizer, clarifier, and questioner; see Palincsar & Brown, 1984) to delve deeper into comprehension.

  - Do text-based writing composition (argumentative, comparative, descriptive, creative).

Assessments

▶ Students' multiliteracy is assessed with multimodal features:

  - Apply the different combinations of assessment modalities—audio, visual, graphic, oral, kinesthetic, and linguistic—by student choice:

    ○ PowerPoints, posters, dramatizations, music

    ○ Self-evaluation and/or team-evaluation rubrics

    ○ Website product, photos, cartoons, graphics

Source: **Adapted from Calderón & Tartaglia (2023); Gottlieb & Calderón (in press).**

What Coaches Do to Support Evidence-Based Instruction: Observing and Coaching Partner Reading

Reflect on the teachers you currently coach. What are the strengths of each teacher? How can you leverage each teacher's strengths to address MLs' reading comprehension needs in a coaching session? How do coaches foster teachers' voices and choices?

Vignette: Partner Reading and Verbal Summaries

Five multilingual students are getting ready for partner reading in Mr. Richards's history class. Luisa and Fabiano are at Level 3 on the district's language test, Rosa Maria and Juan are at Level 2, and Marcos is a newcomer at Level 1 (see Chapter 2, Figure 2.2, for examples of levels of English proficiency). Mr. Richards teamed each ML with a non-ML peer. Marcos is placed in a triad with Fabiano and Henry, who doesn't speak Spanish but volunteered to be in a triad to help Marcos. The whole class is reading aloud in a low voice that only their partners can hear, alternating sentences, and stopping after every paragraph to summarize/retell. Rosa Maria's and Juan's non-ML partners help with fluency when necessary. Luisa's reading is quite fluent, and her summaries have improved. Mr. Richards is monitoring by listening to the fluency of the MLs but also six other students who have low fluency and comprehension skills. They too have reading partners who are fluent readers and skilled at comprehension. The pairs/triads also have on their desks laminated table tents with sentence starters to use for their verbal summaries after each paragraph. During the summaries, they talk about what the paragraph says.
Mr. Richards knows that in a few weeks, they will be discussing at a deeper level what they're reading, maybe arguing, finding evidence and counterevidence, and thinking about how current events information impacts their lives and builds on their knowledge of history.

Coach and Teacher Reflect

After the lesson, the coach asks Mr. Richards how he feels about it. Mr. Richards says he's not happy with Luisa's and Fabiano's progress. They can't seem to move beyond Level 3. He sees that the other MLs are moving forward, even Marcos, the newcomer. The teacher and coach look at the data on the students' discourse during their verbal summaries. They see that Luisa and Fabiano, although quite fluent, use the same basic simple words in phrases instead of sentences. Mr. Richards asks if the coach has seen something like this before and what might be a goal to explore. The coach mentions that he's seen MLs get stuck at Level 3 for a long time and shares a couple of strategies other teachers have used. Coach and teacher discuss each and decide that based on their data, they will ask the ESL specialist to provide a special laminated page with sentence frames instead of sentence starters for Luisa and Fabiano. Along with the tool, they will set this discourse expectation for Luisa and Fabiano to work on for the next two weeks. The students are informed that their teacher, the coach, and the ESL teacher will be listening for those complete sentences. After two weeks, the coach returns to collect data on these and the other MLs. Upon looking at the data, the teacher and coach are elated with the progress the students have made in their verbal discourse.

Although teachers such as Mr. Richards may have recently attended professional development workshops on integrating reading into subject areas, they still need fine-tuning assistance from an ML coach. When teaching reading in the subject areas, teachers will want to know how to build upon students' background knowledge, preteach complex multisyllabic words and sentence frames germane to the subject, provide purposeful fluency-building activities to help students read effortlessly, enable ample peer interaction, and routinely use a set of comprehension-building strategies to help students make sense of the text.

Partner reading has an effect size of $d = 0.75$, and summarization has an effect size of $d = 0.61$. Together they become the most effective way to help all students delve deeper into fluency, prosody, understanding of sentence structures, and comprehension. The combination of partner reading and summarization has been the best approach ($d = 1.20$) at all grade levels (Calderón, 2007). But this combination has to be couched by strategies before, during, and after reading.

These Successful Outcomes Can Be Attained in All Schools!

Teachers new to merging reading, language, and content will need more help from their coach.

What Coaches Do During Reading Instruction

As an ML coach, you can help the teachers prepare the sequence before, during, and after reading. Subsequently, you can observe, gather data, and give teacher feedback. Here is a brisk highlight of the teacher–coach complementing processes. This can be part of your coaching playbook.

Teacher and Coach Plan

1. The teacher (a) provides background knowledge, (b) preteaches at least five keywords, (c) explains objectives, and (d) models reading comprehension strategies.

   The coach observes and documents the four occurrences and student engagement (see Chapter 4 on teaching vocabulary).

2. Students are informed of the *norms of interaction* with partners:

   a. Listen to your partner reading.

   b. Be kind and respectful.

   c. Help one another discover the answer.

   d. Stay on task.

   The coach observes and documents how students adhere to the norms.

3. Partners read aloud alternating sentences, practicing fluency and prosody during and at the end of their sentences. Going sentence by sentence helps MLs learn punctuation stoppers and inflection. Listening to themselves read helps with fluency and prosody

(e.g., pronunciation, intonation, pauses, stresses, punctuation inflection, rate). There is no writing or note-taking during partner reading. Oracy develops a working memory.

The coach observes and documents the flow/fluency of the partner reading and understanding of new vocabulary.

4. Summarization teaches MLs how to select key information, delete what is not important, and paraphrase. Partners stop at the end of each paragraph to reread and tell each other what they understood, point out what information is important to keep in mind, and/or clarify for each other. More formal strategies for summarizing can be taught after a few weeks of answering the informal question, "What does it say in the paragraph?" As noted, there is no writing or note-taking during partner reading because it takes too long and distracts the partners. Plus, students need to develop a working memory.

   The coach observes and documents the quality of the discussion of a paragraph, listening for the use of Tier 2 and 3 words (described in Chapter 4), accuracy of the content, and engagement. The teacher monitors and also takes notes.

5. After reading two or three paragraphs, partners go back and review and restate important points. An option is for students to write one- or two-sentence summaries.

   The coach observes and documents the understanding of the whole section the students have been reading and discussing. The teacher monitors as they summarize and discuss the whole segment.

6. The teacher leads a whole-class discussion with a few points on the board.

   The coach observes the class discussion using a seating chart to document who responds and how many responses are generated with what type of questions.

The coach shares a clean version of the notes, the seating chart with tabulations for speakers during the class discussion, and the type of questions that generated the most interest and discussion. These data will also serve to set up the next coaching observation and feedback session to reinforce what works for partner reading and summarization and what needs to be tweaked and how.

What Coaches Do: Use Notes or a Checklist for Observing Partner Reading

Because it is the foundation for the four language domains, teachers need to make sure students learn how to do partner reading and summarization well. It requires speaking, listening, reading (and remembering the content), and later writing. A coach can take notes guided by the sequential statements in the previous section. Alternatively, the coach can use the checklist in Figure 3.1 to plan a preconference where the coach and teacher plan the observation, and later use it to record the observation. The coach can use a check mark in the first column if an action is observed, describe the action in the second column, and take notes in the third. Some coaches and teachers prefer to use a numeric score of 1 to 4, with 4 being excellent. Other coaches and teachers prefer noting the time sequence for each teaching/learning action.

Figure 3.1 Checklist for Observing Partner Reading

✓ CHECK OR USE 1–4 OR RECORD TIME OF OBSERVATION	LEARNING ACTION	OBSERVATION NOTES
	Partners are sitting close together, text in hand, and ready to start reading.	
	They read aloud alternating sentences for fluency and prosody: • Pronunciation • Intonation • Pauses • Stresses • Punctuation • Inflection • Emphasis of keywords • Rhythm • Pace	
	They help each other if necessary (record some of their reading challenges and ways of working them out).	

✓ CHECK *OR* USE 1–4 *OR* RECORD TIME OF OBSERVATION	LEARNING ACTION	OBSERVATION NOTES
	Students adhere to the social-emotional learning (SEL) or interaction norms the teacher has required.	
	They stop after every paragraph and summarize what they read using Tier 2 and 3 vocabulary (see Chapter 4) and demonstrate comprehension of each paragraph.	
	After reading and summarizing, partners form teams of four to formulate questions, or work on cognitive or graphic organizers.	
	Partners actively participate in the whole-class discussion.	
	Partners use a rubric or self-evaluation protocol to reflect on their SEL competencies, performance during reading, and understanding of the text.	
	Partners choose from different combinations of assessment modalities—audio, visual, graphic, oral, kinesthetic, or linguistic—to present to the class.	

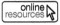 Available for download at http://resources.corwin.com/CMLExcellence

Teacher and Coach Monitor and Make Notations on Seating Charts

There are two different seating configurations to consider for observation. When students are sitting in rows, the coach and teacher can walk up and down the rows, as shown in Figure 3.2A, to assist and/or take notes for later reflection. When the students are sitting in teams, such as in Figure 3.2B, the teacher and coach can move between teams.

Figure 3.2 Data Collection on Student Interaction

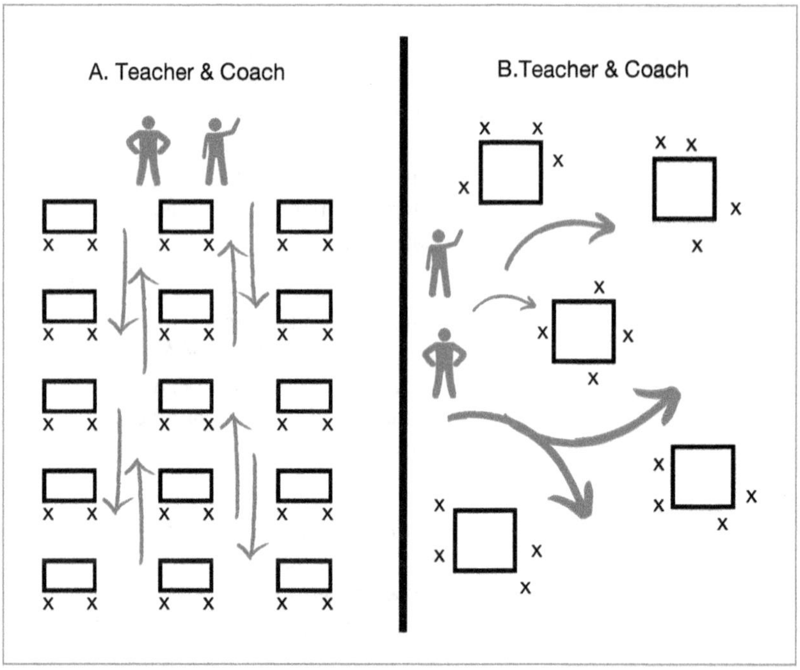

Source: Graphic by Leticia M. Trower

The Instructional Model: After-Reading Activities to Consolidate Vocabulary, Reading Comprehension, and Content Mastery

After students have engaged in partner reading for fluency and use of new vocabulary and pondered the information in the text, a second round of reading activities helps to develop close reading strategies. This sequence is particularly valuable when students are confronted with complex text such as a historical event, mathematical problems, rules and regulations for basketball, charts, digital media, graphs, or the traditional literature piece that calls for higher-order thinking or making inferences.

After-reading activities also show how students are applying their new knowledge and where some gaps might exist. In this phase, students can now write using graphic organizers, two-column notes, team concept maps, PowerPoints, and other multimodal information displays.

Close analytic reading integrates many of the elements that are needed to support MLs in meeting the standards. Close reading incorporates many academic language, reading comprehension, and writing objectives in one set of activities that facilitate analytic reading. Formulating questions and team activities help students raise their own standards as well (Calderón & Tartaglia, 2023).

Recursive Reading Using Academic Language

One of our favorite largest-evidence strategies is formulating questions ($d = 0.80$). Student-formulated questions are a follow-up consolidation activity that takes students back into the text to do *close reading*. They need to deeply comprehend a text to write questions. If students are only answering teacher or book questions, it can become an easy routine where students don't have to do much thinking. On the other hand, when students write questions for other teams to answer, they strive for accuracy and difficulty. Writing questions in teams helps students to analyze the author's craft and identify key points, details, and text structures. Besides, competing with other teams to write questions creates high levels of cooperation and fun competition within and between teams.

Vignette: After Reading

After partner reading and summarizing, Mr. Richards asks the students to work in teams of four to formulate questions. He distributes index cards and asks the teams to write two questions per team and write the question on the front of the card and the answer (or possible answer if it is an open question) on the back. Facts can come from the text or background knowledge. They are to select and write their team's name on the card. When finished, the cards are collected by Mr. Richards to use in a cooperative-competitive strategy. Students number from 1 to 4 in each team. Mr. Richards reads a question and gives two minutes for all the teams to come up with an answer and make sure that all the students are prepared to answer for their team. He then arbitrarily calls a number. All the students with that number stand, and each one gives the team's answer. A student from the

(Continued)

(Continued)

*next team must build on the previous answer. Mr. Richards likes
this strategy because it builds individual accountability since
each student must be prepared to answer for the team. Therefore,
he assigns MLs to different teams and reviews the norms of team
interaction so that all students work together effectively to help
each other and build team accountability. The team that wrote
the question gets to give positive feedback on the academic
language used by the respondents.*

Coach and Teacher Reflect

*Mr. Richards had asked the coach to observe and record how well
he gives directions for conducting the cooperative-competitive
activity. The last time he tried it, the students were confused and
didn't know who was supposed to represent the team and answer
when Mr. Richards read a question that another team had written.
This time, Mr. Richards wanted to video record the lesson so he
could play it back for their analysis. As they reviewed the video,
Mr. Richards moaned and said, "I did it again! I mean I didn't do
it—I forgot to tell the students to number off in their teams. That
way I could call a number, say 3, and only they would respond
when I called on each team. They were kind enough to appoint
a speaker, and that student answered each time. But I wanted
all four students to have a turn, especially the MLs." The coach
suggested having numbers 1 to 4 written on separate pieces
of paper, folded, and placed in a small basket on his table. That
would be a reminder to have the students number off and a way to
"blindly" select a folded paper with a number on it. Mr. Richards
would be sure to call all four numbers during the activity.*

What Coaches Do Before and During an Observation on Formulating Questions

It's the teacher's voice and choice! The checklist in Figure 3.3 can be
used for a preconference where the coach and teacher plan the observation. The teacher selects the segment they will be teaching and tells the
coach the time frame to come to observe that segment. The teacher also
states the concern or focus during that segment (e.g., student discourse,
team interaction, time spent, teacher delivery). The coach and teacher
agree on the type of data collection and/or method for gathering the data
(e.g., checklist, notes, video, other).

Figure 3.3 Observing and Coaching Question Formulation and Cooperative-Competitive

✓ CHECK *OR* USE 1–4 *OR* RECORD TIMES FOR EACH	LEARNING ACTIONS	NOTES
	All partners are working together to write questions at a teacher-assigned level of Bloom or other taxonomies.	
	There are rich discussions in teams of four, and they use the Tier 2 and 3 words (see Chapter 4) and facts from the text.	
	They go back into the text to find evidence and refine their questions. (You might want to collect samples of questions to share with the teacher during feedback and reflection.)	
	During the cooperative-competitive activity, they respond in complete sentences. (Make notations of sample discourse.)	
	When each team responds and builds on the previous student response, they use connectors such as "I politely disagree because on page . . ." or "I agree with Team X since . . . Moreover, . . ."	
	Other observations.	

online resources Available for download at http://resources.corwin.com/CMLExcellence

Observing Newcomers

Some newcomers, dually identified students who need special education and ESL support, or struggling/striving readers will benefit from foundational reading skills. Either a reading teacher or an ESL/English language development (ELD) teacher can help with the alphabetic principle, phonemic awareness, phonological awareness, basic vocabulary, decoding skills, spelling, reading fluency, and beginning comprehension strategies. Nonetheless, newcomers can still participate in partner reading and after-reading activities.

What Coaches Do to Support a Newcomer

When observing classrooms with newcomers, you can use the same checklists for vocabulary shared in Chapter 4 and in this chapter (see Figures 3.3, 3.4, 4.8, 4.13, and 4.16). For ESL/ELD or special education co-teachers, Figure 3.4 will help with observation and giving feedback on the section the teacher selects. You might want to turn this into a checklist or a rubric for your observations.

Figure 3.4   A Teaching and Coaching Sequence for Beginning Multilingual Readers

1. **Engagement and motivation:** The teacher uses texts that reflect the students' culture or their interests in the new culture.

2. **Social-emotional learning:** The teacher presents a strategy for developing routines and behaviors, tackling difficulty, or overcoming learning barriers.

3. **Print conventions:** The teacher presents the alphabet, left-to-right reading, spaces, and letter formation.

4. **Phonics:** The teacher preteaches phonemic awareness, word meanings, and decoding words from the text the students are about to read.

5. **Vocabulary:** The teacher preteaches five words that will help students to comprehend the text they are about to read.

6. **Fluency modeling:** The teacher reads a paragraph aloud to students as they track what the teacher is reading.

7. **Fluency practice:** The teacher does choral reading with students on that same paragraph. The teacher reads again, and newcomers do "shadow reading" in soft voices as they try to keep up with the teacher's prosody.

8. **Comprehension strategy:** The teacher does a think-aloud to demonstrate a reading strategy key to comprehending the text features or text structures.

9. **Reading approach—fluency and comprehension:** The teacher sets up partner reading where students read aloud, alternating sentences to practice fluency, and then summarize aloud together after each paragraph for comprehension. The teacher demonstrates or explains the social-emotional competencies that will help partners be successful readers.

10. **Comprehension and discourse:** The teacher debriefs with the whole class (important information, words students are not sure of, and what they have learned so far).

11. **Grammar and spelling:** The teacher provides explicit instruction on selected sentence structures: length, punctuation, complexity, passive voice, affixes, and author's craft.

12. **Depth of comprehension:** The students return to the text in pairs or teams to formulate questions from the text, instead of answering questions from the text.

13. **Depth of comprehension and content mastery:** The students use their student-formulated questions to test their peers in exciting activities.

14. **Development of metacognitive skills and strategies:** The teacher models a strategy for higher-order thinking during text analysis by using increasingly complex original and authentic texts that are appealing and relevant to adolescent learners.

15. **Writing, editing, revising, and creativity:** Students write using the content they have learned using a variety of genres (art, compositions, letters, interviews, flyers, PowerPoint, etc.) for a real audience.

16. **Translanguaging:** Multilingual students are encouraged to use their home language during summarizing, formulating questions, writing assignments, and asking peers for clarification (see Chapter 4 for more information on translanguaging).

17. **Multimodal performance assessment:** The teacher or students use multimodalities to demonstrate learning, record student performance on as many components of this list as possible, and gauge their learning progress (adapted from Calderón, 2007).

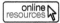 Available for download at http://resources.corwin.com/CMLExcellence

Newcomers can also summarize with the same routine. For a couple of weeks, newcomers listen and whisper as they repeat some of the words, shadow reading what they hear from their partners. Eventually, they begin to contribute some detail to the summary as they build confidence. After a few more weeks, they will take a formal turn as part of the triad summary where two peers continue to help as necessary (see Figure 3.5).

Figure 3.5 Triad Reading for Newcomers

1. **The newcomer (NC) sits in the middle of two higher-level MLs or native English speakers (S1 and S2).**

2. **When S1 reads a sentence, NC tracks and whisper reads the same sentence.**

3. **When S2 reads a sentence, NC whisper reads along.**

4. **Eventually, when NC is ready, the reading is done:**

   S1 → NC → S2 → NC → S1 → NC → S2 → NC

5. **This gives NC double turns during each cycle.**

 Available for download at http://resources.corwin.com/CMLExcellence

Newcomers can also participate in the question formulation and cooperative-competitive activities. The team members help the newcomer get ready to respond in case their number is called.

Newcomers need to start talking, reading, and writing from the first day they enter a classroom. It behooves the newcomers' teachers to establish norms for their classmates so they can help make a safe place where the newcomers feel comfortable and confident trying and making mistakes. Mistakes are natural, normal, and necessary if they (or us) are to grow.

You're not a reading coach; you're a comprehension coach!

The Instructional Model: Social-Emotional Learning Strategies That Support Reading

The Collaborative for Academic, Social, and Emotional Learning (CASEL, n.d.) identifies five competencies that address the process through which young people and adults acquire and apply knowledge, skills, and attitudes to develop healthy identities, manage emotions, achieve personal and collective goals, feel and show empathy for others, establish and maintain supportive relationships, and make responsible and caring decisions (https://casel.org/fundamentals-of-sel/).

Social-emotional learning (SEL) is easily applied during reading. SEL helps MLs learn cognitive and emotional self-regulation, prosocial behavior, problem solving, and conflict resolution—competencies that are very useful as MLs learn to interact with a new culture during all the reading and learning activities. The teachers review or display posters of the norms of interaction or competencies that will help students succeed during reading and after-reading activities.

The following summarizes the five key competencies of SEL and how they relate to MLs' reading process:

- ✓ **Self-awareness** is the ability to understand one's emotions, thoughts, and values that influence behavior across situations. During partner reading and summarization, students must be aware of their own feelings about talking with another student and portray the right attitude.

- ✓ **Self-management** is the ability to understand one's emotions to achieve one's goals and aspirations. For partner reading and summarization, pairs must control feelings to focus on rereading and jointly building a summary of what they read. They need to remind each other that using the new words to summarize is part of the task.

✓ **Social awareness** is the ability to understand and empathize with others, especially those from diverse social and cultural backgrounds, English proficiencies, and emotional states. During partner reading and summarization, peers use positive talk, do not get distracted, and help one another.

✓ **Relationship skills** are the ability to establish and maintain healthy and supportive relationships and to effectively navigate settings with diverse individuals and groups. Partners must be open to creating a relationship of trust, respect, and friendly communication to complete the tasks that require cognitive assonance.

✓ **Responsible decision making** is the ability to make caring and constructive choices about personal behavior and social interactions across settings. During all the learning activities in reading, remembering, and recognizing key ideas for summarizing, peers must make decisions as to what information to keep and what to discard. One of the most important decisions we need to help them commit to is coming to school and attending each class every day. Students cannot learn if they are absent.

What Coaches Do to Observe and Support Social-Emotional Learning

Using the preceding examples, the Teacher and Coach Reflection and Checklist that follows can be used when a teacher asks a coach to observe how they explain a specific SEL competency and/or how students apply that competency during a specific reading segment. We want students to always participate in active learning where they develop listening, speaking, reading, and writing skills—all the while learning to apply self-management, self-awareness, social awareness, relationship, and responsible decision-making skills. Another way of looking at SEL competencies from a reading research perspective is to think of them as *executive function (EF) skills*.

EF skills are higher-order self-regulatory neurocognitive processes recruited particularly in complex, goal-directed tasks. EFs include three core skills—cognitive flexibility, working memory, and inhibitory control—and skills such as attention and planning (Dawson & Guare, 2018; Diamond, 2013). For second-language learners, these core skills or competencies must be taught in every classroom (Calderón, 2007).

When students are reading with their partners, they will be practicing SEL/EF skills or competencies. The following list can serve as a teacher–coach planning tool, an observation-data-gathering tool for feedback, or a checklist for students to practice self-regulation.

Vignette: Social-Emotional Learning and Executive Function

Mr. Richards wants his coach to use the checklist of social-emotional learning and executive function skills (pages 99 & 100) and focus on which of the interpersonal/intrapersonal skills his students are applying. Mr. Richards has given this part of the list to the students and explained what each skill looks like when students are formulating questions. The teacher and coach agree that tabulating each competency would be the best way to collect data.

Teacher and Coach Reflection and Checklist

The coach presents data on the team where one Level 2 ML and one Level 3 ML have been assigned with two non-MLs. The coach has tabulated each skill as follows:

- ☐ *Intentionality and mindfulness:* ~~HHI~~ ~~HHI~~
- ☐ *Listening skills:* ~~HHI~~ ~~HHI~~ ~~HHI~~ ~~HHI~~
- ☐ *Speaking skills:* ~~HHI~~ ~~HHI~~ III
- ☐ *Sharing text ideas:* ~~HHI~~ II
- ☐ *Sharing reading strategies:* II
- ☐ *Conflict resolution skills:* III

As coach and teacher analyze the data, Mr. Richards is delighted that the students are listening to their peers, speaking more, and sharing ideas and even a couple of reading strategies. The coach says that there was an instance of disagreement but gave the team points for being mindful of others' feelings and making a deliberate attempt to resolve that disagreement.

Checklist of Social-Emotional Learning and Executive Function Skills to Practice During Reading

Interpersonal/Intrapersonal Skills

- ☐ Intentionality and mindfulness

- ☐ Listening skills

- ☐ Speaking skills

- ☐ Sharing text ideas

- ☐ Sharing reading strategies

- ☐ Conflict resolution skills

Cognitive Growth: Metacognition

- ☐ Working memory—keeping information in mind

- ☐ Using new information

- ☐ Developing confidence as a reader

- ☐ Monitoring comprehension

- ☐ Building knowledge of content

Attitude

- ☐ Attentional control

- ☐ Inhibitory control

- ☐ Motivation and engagement—willingness to try

- ☐ Accepting and giving help

Some teachers prefer notes and will request a chart such as Figure 3.6.

Figure 3.6 Social-Emotional Learning Notes on Observations

SEL COMPETENCY	NOTES: TEACHER INSTRUCTIONS	NOTES: STUDENT APPLICATION
Self-awareness		
Self-management		
Social awareness		
Relationship skills		
Responsible decision making		
Quality of learning in pairs or teams		
Learning goals achieved		
Shared and celebrated success!		

online resources Available for download at http://resources.corwin.com/CMLExcellence

EF is so important to reading that there is reason to believe that for some students, limited EF skills are the primary cause of reading difficulty (Duke et al., 2021).

An Activity for You

What other SEL/EF skills/competencies are MLs using during partner reading?

The Instructional Model: Cooperative Learning—From Pairs and Triads to Teamwork

When forming groups, spread the wealth. The way teachers group students for team learning makes all the difference in learning. An ML (Figure 3.7A) ought to be in different teams of four with high-level (B), average (C), and striving (D) readers. The exception is when a newcomer arrives late in the year. The newcomer can be twinned with a same-language bilingual student if possible, and the team of four becomes five. The newcomer will need support by someone who speaks the same language for at least a few weeks. Afterward, the newcomer can be placed with nonbilingual students who will be empathetic and willing to facilitate comprehension. This is where an SEL lesson can help all students become more conscientious of others and learn to communicate in a global world.

Sometimes you will want students to work in different pairs. It can start with MLs (A) and average readers (C), and partners can switch every two weeks or when a new unit creates a natural break. When students are ready to move to after-reading activities, working in teams facilitates that learning. Hattie (2009) found that cooperative learning ($d = 0.59$) engenders more student discourse ($d = 0.82$) when supported by direct instruction. We totally agree that cooperative learning is the best context for MLs' discourse development, especially when MLs are heterogeneously grouped as seen in Figure 3.7.

Figure 3.7 Team Formation

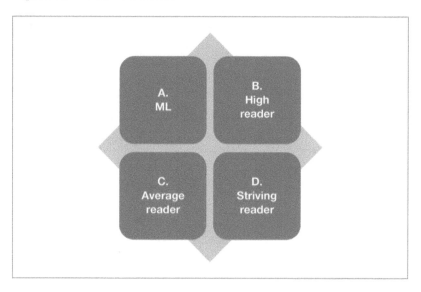

Discourse Patterns for Cooperative Learning

For cooperative learning to flow smoothly, teachers might review the SEL competencies (self-management, self-awareness, social awareness, relationship skills, and responsible decision-making skills) or enact social norms of interaction during teamwork. Social norms are usually posted in classrooms as shown in Figure 3.8.

Figure 3.8 Team Norms

> ✓ Be respectful of your peers.
>
> ✓ Contribute ideas.
>
> ✓ Accept others' ideas.
>
> ✓ Disagree politely.
>
> ✓ Complete your tasks.
>
> ✓ Learn!

Some teachers prefer not to post and instead have the norms on the students' desks or in their folders. Proximity enables more use. Table tents are other tools a coach might suggest distributing to the teams before they begin their tasks. These can have the vocabulary of the week, sentence starters, transition words, or any reminders of the discourse the students are to use. A table tent can have several charts with vocabulary, sentence starters, or sentence frames such as those shown in Figure 3.9. This tool helps MLs use the discourse protocols for agreeing and disagreeing during the cooperative-competitive activity.

Figure 3.9 Polite Discourse During Peer Discussions

IF YOU AGREE	IF YOU DISAGREE
• I agree . . .	• I disagree . . .
• I agree, and I would like to add . . .	• I respectfully disagree . . .
• I want to echo . . .	• I disagree due to . . .
• I concur . . .	• However, the author states . . .
• Moreover, . . .	• On the other hand, . . .
• Furthermore, . . .	• Conversely, in the text, . . .

Two other ExC-ELL discourse tools are those that would help MLs talk more and express their opinions. Simple sentence starters such as the ones shown in Figure 3.10 and the notation strategies shown in Figure 3.11 help to guide their discussions or note-taking.

Figure 3.10 Sentence Starters

- This is about . . .
- That character reminds me of . . .
- That part reminds me of . . .
- I liked the . . .
- I need help understanding . . .

Now Students Can Write or Make Notations

Up to now, most of the responses from students have been verbal—oral ping-pong during the vocabulary Step 6 (see Chapter 4, page 134), oral partner reading, oral summaries of each paragraph during partner reading, and class debriefings/discussions. Now that students have read and can write questions, they might want to use notation strategies for annotating on the margins a reflection, an opinion, a question, a theme, the gist, or a quick summary. A teacher can post and show how to use symbols such as those in Figure 3.11.

Figure 3.11 Coding for Readers

- **E** = evidence
- ✔ = important
- ★ = main idea
- ♥ = my favorite

These tools can be added to the table tents for all in a team to see and use. You will find table tents that can be downloaded from www.exc-ell.com.

What Coaches Do During Cooperative Learning Activities

A teacher might ask the coach to observe student engagement during cooperative learning activities such as Tea Party or Concentric Circles (Calderón, 1995). This activity helps peers verbally review key information before an exam. The teacher can call out several questions, then give students one minute to discuss the answer to each.

Tea Party or Concentric Circles

- Have students stand in two circles, facing each other.

- Ask the first question, then give students one minute to discuss the answer with the classmate directly opposite them.

- After one minute, call on volunteers to share their answers with the group.

- Subsequently have the inner circle shift clockwise.

- Read the second question and give the new pairs a minute to discuss.

- Repeat the activity until they've had a chance to answer all the questions.

- Finally, have students write their answers to the questions. Or if you prefer, assign the questions as homework.

- An alternative is to have students stand in two straight lines, and one keeps moving down.

Other After-Reading or Center Activities

Students can work in pairs, in teams, or individually on these activities to anchor content knowledge, vocabulary, or reading comprehension.

Vignette: Cooperative Learning

"I tried cooperative learning once or twice, but it turned into a madhouse! I'm afraid to try it again," said Mrs. Harris. Her coach listened attentively as she described the "madhouse" incident. Then, the coach showed Mrs. Harris Figure 3.12, and they discussed each section with the questions she posed. After going

back to reread this chapter, Mrs. Harris decided she was going to ask students to work in triads (because it seemed easier for her to manage small teams) to do a cognitive map of the science chapter they were reading. They had already done partner reading and summarization. Since she was starting from scratch, she asked her coach to use Figure 3.13 and focus on numbers 1, 2, and 3.

Teacher and Coach Reflection

Before presenting the data, the coach asked Mrs. Harris how she felt about her lesson. She excitedly replied that it went so much better than expected—that the students followed her directions, and all seemed to be on task. The coach gave her reassurance and congratulated her on a great start. They began to discuss the next steps, but then Mrs. Harris noticed something not so satisfactory: "My ELs were not as involved as I would want them to be. I thought they would enjoy this." The coach said, "I noticed that too. Let's discuss that and come up with a strategy for next time. You have already conquered the steps and social interaction, so let's look at the academic language and discourse for MLs as our next goal."

Figure 3.12   Anchoring Activities to Integrate Language, Literacy, and Content

- Cognitive or semantic mapping of what students read
- Content/story retelling using new vocabulary
- Writing sentences like those in the text
- Finding words with multiple meanings or cognates with home language
- Pronunciation practice
- Fluency practice
- Content-related writing
- Reflections on emotions and relationships
- Meeting with same home-language buddies to clarify or create knowledge in their primary language, using translanguaging, or in the language of their choice

Figure 3.13 Coaching Cooperative Learning

COOPERATIVE LEARNING FEATURES	TEACHER PRESENTATION	STUDENT APPLICATION
1. Heterogeneous teams are formed, and students waste no time to start learning.		
2. Students use the social skills taught for this learning activity.		
3. Students help each other stay on task, and all contribute to the learning of the intended content.		
4. Students use Tier 2 and 3 words (see Chapter 4) from the text and SEL discourse.		
5. Students assess self- and team cooperation and learning.		

online resources Available for download at http://resources.corwin.com/CMLExcellence

Focusing on Comprehension Skills

Shanahan's (2005) table for developing comprehension strategies has been adapted in Figure 3.14 for ML coaches by adding ExC-ELL characteristics. Shanahan's description of *question-asking* pertains to students asking themselves questions. However, the same strategies can be used by MLs to learn how to ask questions when working in teams with more proficient peers.

Figure 3.14 Observation and Coaching Protocol for Reading Comprehension

READING COMPREHENSION SKILL *CIRCLE THE SPECIFIC FEATURES OBSERVED	NOTES ON TEACHER PRESENTATION	NOTES ON STUDENT APPLICATION
Monitors own reading (e.g., read-aloud, partner reading, team reading)		
Attention to text features (e.g., titles, subtitles, headings, bold print, color print, print size, maps, diagrams, graphs, charts)		
Attention to text structures (e.g., cause and effect, problem and solution, sequential, claims, counterclaims, descriptive, persuasive, argumentative, compare and contrast, inferences, evidence)		
Summarizes or synthesizes verbally or in writing		
Identifies author's purpose, main idea, character traits, events, sequence, and plot		
Engages in question-asking (e.g., who, what, why, where, how); questions the text/author		
Uses graphic organizers or cognitive maps		

Source: Adapted from Shanahan (2005).

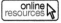 Available for download at http://resources.corwin.com/CMLExcellence

Transfer Between Languages (Cross-Linguistic and Cognitive Transfer)

Some students have the benefit of participating in dual-language programs where they receive instruction in both their home language and English so the linguistic intersection accelerates learning of both languages. While there is still a dearth of empirical studies about dual-language instruction, there is ample evidence of cross-linguistic transfer of some reading skills. Knowledge of which skills transfer from one language to the other accelerates reading comprehension. Foundational skills development can call attention to the similarities and differences between specific features of English and students' home languages. Whereas foundational (phonics or decoding) skills vary in two languages, metacognitive skills (thinking about thinking) and comprehension strategies are more transferable (Calderón & Montenegro, 2021).

Cross-linguistic and cross-metacognitive comprehension skills that transfer include making inferences and identifying cause and effect or problem and solution. The comprehension monitoring skills that students acquire in their first language can be applied to reading comprehension in their new language (Moats, 2020).

Therefore, biliteracy instruction builds on concepts learned across languages and promotes metalinguistic awareness and metacognitive skills. When possible, teachers can explicitly teach students to develop and apply cross-linguistic understandings. One thing to keep in mind is that making predictions and inferences will be difficult for MLs because they might not possess sufficient topical knowledge and the vocabulary to make them explicit.

Some teachers might want a coach to observe how they highlight grammatical, decoding, or metacognitive skills to assist comprehension. The teacher should also explain the purpose and intended outcome of that instructional event.

As you will see in Chapter 4, Step 5 of the seven-step process also serves to introduce an aspect of grammatical functions (e.g., parts of speech, polysemous words, affixes, cognates, and other word characteristics). The seven-step process can be used to point out morphological similarities and differences: for example, *magic* and *mágico* or contrasting morphemes across languages such as *investigation and investigación*. (See Chapter 4 for examples of cognates).

To go deeper into grammar, teachers can select two or three sentences from the text to highlight how sentences convey meaning. Pointing out some sentence features such as parts of speech, punctuation, sentence parts, morphology, and types of sentences will also help comprehension. If possible, the core content teacher or a bilingual teacher can help compare and contrast the different features of the student's home language and English.

Some examples of differences between Spanish and English are as follows:

- They have a similar alphabet, but letters are pronounced differently.

▶ Punctuation is slightly different: *¿Qué? / What?*

▶ Cognates have similar spelling and pronunciation: *photosynthesis / fotosíntesis.*

▶ There are nontransferable or false cognates: *dime* (10 cents) / *dime* (tell me).

▶ There are nonexisting graphemes: use of apostrophes such as *'s* or *s'* in English and use of *ñ* and accent marks (José) in Spanish.

▶ Metalinguistic skills are the same: phonology, orthography, morphology, semantics, syntactics, grammar, and pragmatics.

A coach can observe that interaction, take notes, share, and discuss the observation notes. A plan can be jointly constructed to use the next time a similar lesson is needed.

Tips for Teachers

✓ Parse any test questions—how many words will be difficult to understand?

✓ What is culturally unfamiliar in a test question that explicitly centers on white culture?

✓ What grammatical inaccuracies repeatedly appear in student verbal and written discourse?

The Instructional Model: Self-Evaluation and Performance Assessment Strategy

Another aspect of active self-regulation is the use of reading comprehension strategies (Duke et al., 2021). We want to make sure that students practice with peers and use the many strategies that teachers have taught. For example, using exit tickets, group work, or centers, MLs can practice with peers how to do any of the following, and an ML coach can record the language and reading progressions:

1. Use the new words in your own sentence stem.

2. Map out the seven-step strategy (described in Chapter 4) for a new word or phrase.

3. Analyze morphemes in a sentence or paragraph.

4. Look for cognates (you will read more about cognates in Chapter 4).

5. Look up meanings of polysemous words or idioms.

6. Make inferences from a new paragraph.

7. Write a rulebook with all the strategies the teachers have taught about reading and word knowledge.

8. Make a cognitive map of the text or a vocabulary map.

9. Use media, posters, PowerPoints, dramatic plays, and other creative ways to demonstrate strategies 1–8 and other EF and SEL skills learned.

What Coaches Do to Enhance the Reading Process

Coaches can help teachers review student work and jointly develop criteria for individual student products in collegial teams.

Scenarios for Collegial Discussions in Learning Communities

Coaches in their coaches' learning communities (CLCs) or teachers and coaches in teacher learning communities (TLCs) cut the scenarios in Figure 3.15 into cards. Each participant takes a card and shares what that scenario might look like and the type of feedback a coach might give, or what feedback the teacher might want to receive if this ever occurred. Creative minds will likely come up with an educational game.

Figure 3.15   Role-Play Cards for Teachers and Coaches

Coop Learning	Coop Learning	Coop Learning	Reading
Teacher did not monitor student groups during activity.	Teacher did not model expected outcome for activity or reading.	Instructions are not written or posted for students to refer to as they work.	Teacher did not read aloud/think aloud with self-correcting strategies.
Reading	**Reading**	**Reading**	**Reading**
Students doing paired reading did not alternate sentences or listen to each other.	Students did not stop to summarize what they read after each paragraph.	Teacher's read-aloud is too long.	Teacher forgets to identify the comprehension skill for students to work on during reading.
Vocabulary	**Vocabulary**	**Vocabulary**	**Vocabulary**
Forgot to focus on grammar, cognate, or other element that highlights the word (see Step 7 in Chapter 4).	Spent more than 10–15 minutes per day on vocabulary.	Omitted interactive practice (see Step 6 in Chapter 4).	Didn't get enough responses from multiple students to ensure 100% participation.

Think About It

What if the elementary schools with MLs also adopt evidence-based instruction and whole-school comprehensive professional development models? Would that prevent having so many LTELs in middle and high schools?

To Summarize

▶ Reading instruction integrated into all subjects is critical for MLs and all other striving readers.

▶ Reading comprehension is the product of vocabulary knowledge.

▶ MLs must speak, listen, read, and write from day one in each class with the right support.

▶ Texts for MLs must be challenging, high interest, and at grade level.

▶ There must be a balance between foundational reading skills and reading comprehension skills for beginning-level MLs. Teaching phonics alone does not work. Spending too much time on phonics doesn't work either.

▶ Social-emotional competencies can be integrated into vocabulary, reading, and after-reading instruction.

▶ Reading failure is unnecessary; for over twenty years we have known from scientific panels and empirical studies what works with MLs (August & Shanahan, 2006, 2008; Calderón, 2007; Short & Fitzsimmons, 2007).

▶ Without coaches, about 75–95 percent of the teachers in a school will stop using the new instructional strategies.

Recommendations for the Whole School to Enact

▶ Prioritize reading proficiency for every student.

▶ Establish nurturing environments where MLs can display their talents and flourish.

▶ Establish an integrated framework of language, literacy, SEL, and core content in all classrooms.

▶ Address foundational reading needs of the neediest with evidence-based programs specific for MLs.

- Provide professional development for everyone in the school for skill development, positive disposition, equity, and quality implementation of new evidence-based reading instructional strategies.

- Provide ongoing coaching.

- Eliminate ineffective structures and instructional practices that prevent quality implementation.

- Provide more time for teachers to study, prepare, and share with colleagues.

- Share these new approaches to MLs' success and well-being with their families and provide a voice for them in this process.

- Leverage policy and funding.

- Promote accountability, monitor, and celebrate effective implementation.

- Use data for continuous improvement.

What Coaches Do: Whole-School Transformation of Reading

Many states are now requiring reading coaches to have depth of knowledge of evidence-based reading as recommended by literacy panels (August & Shanahan, 2006, 2008; National Reading Panel, 2000)—phonemic awareness, phonics, fluency, vocabulary, and comprehension—and knowledge on how to work with striving readers. Coaches can assist a school to set a climate for MLs and all readers to thrive beginning with these helping actions:

- Help interpret data from reading assessments and apply it to reading improvement strategies and effective ways to teach writing.

- Help understand the evidence-based components of reading and which ones individual MLs need to work on.

- Help develop a common language about reading for MLs.

- Help teachers and administrators know what they don't know about MLs.

Figure 3.16 summarizes the key messages from this chapter.

Figure 3.16   A Vision of Literacy and Biliteracy for MLs

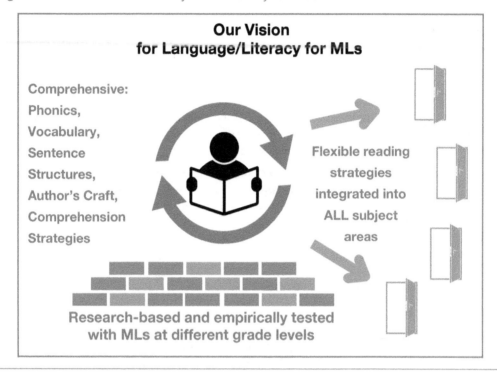

Source: Graphic by Leticia M. Trower

Message From a Special Guest: Coaching Through Noticings and Wonderings

By Andrea Honigsfeld

Whenever I have the opportunity to work as a coach in a classroom that serves MLs, I immediately communicate to the educators (teachers, paraprofessionals, other coaches, and administrators) what an honor and privilege it is for me to be in that learning space. I also share simple yet clear expectations including boundaries for myself.

My most effective coaching strategy is a very simple formula that creates a nonjudgmental, nonevaluative opportunity for me to be a visitor in the classroom by simply taking notes on my "noticings and wonderings." In other words, I share with the teachers whose classes I am about to visit that I am there to support them; to notice everything that is going well in support of MLs; to capture examples of how the students are responding to instruction linguistically, academically, and socioemotionally; and to point out what practices yield the most promising immediate and long-term outcomes. In addition, I anticipate that I will have some authentic questions in the form of wonderings: What do I notice that I am curious about? What would I like to learn more about? What questions emerge that I truly do not have an answer to?

(Continued)

(Continued)

Once this protocol is established, it is easy for the teacher(s) whose classroom(s) I visited to also share their noticings and wonderings. We compare notes: Did we notice the same things about the students? Do the teachers have a question or wondering that I might be able to answer by offering a new perspective? Using this noticings and wonderings protocol, by design the postvisit debrief becomes a powerful opportunity for collaborative conversations, shared explorations, and lots of celebrations of both student and teacher learning.

Andrea Honigsfeld, PhD, is a professor in the School of Education and Human Services at Molloy College in Rockville Centre, New York. She is a well-known author and consultant of co-teaching approaches.

From One Coach to Another

Coaching vocabulary with ExC-ELL has been an incredibly enjoyable and rewarding experience. I have vivid memories of working with a ninth-grade English class comprised of MLs. This was a sheltered class with over twenty students learning English. The teacher's goal was to engage the students in reading Romeo and Juliet *together, but the text was challenging, and she was concerned the students would have difficulty comprehending it. While we managed to find various versions of the text at different reading levels, including a graphic novel adaptation, it was evident that many of the vocabulary words were unfamiliar to the students. To address this, I worked closely with the teacher to parse the text by dividing it into manageable sections for the students. We also handpicked several Tier 2 and 3 words (see Chapter 4) to introduce to the students before delving into the reading material.*

As part of the daily routine, the teacher would utilize the ExC-ELL seven-step process (outlined in Chapter 4) to explore five to seven vocabulary words before having the students read the text. This approach allowed the students to develop a deeper understanding of the selected vocabulary and provided a solid foundation for their subsequent partner reading activities and oral summarizations. To further reinforce their comprehension, the students actively participated in reading response and writing activities. The teacher encouraged them to incorporate the newly learned vocabulary words into their discussions about the text, their exit passes, and all other reading and writing assignments.

One assignment was the scene where the characters attend the masquerade ball. The teacher pretaught the word masquerade, and then she used that word to teach the figurative and literal meanings of mask through the characters. Also, most of the students were Spanish speaking, so when she taught the seven steps, she pointed out the Spanish cognate, la mascarada, and the students were able to make the connection to further their understanding of the word. They later created masks that they thought each character would wear based on what they had learned about them.

To say that the teacher was astonished by the students' ability to read and comprehend the text would be an understatement. It was truly a remarkable experience to witness the students engaging in thoughtful conversations about the text while skillfully utilizing the vocabulary words they had learned. This transformative journey of understanding the text captivated both the students and the teacher. Although the teacher had previously taught ninth-grade English, witnessing these students' genuine comprehension and their excitement in engaging with the text was a sight she had never seen before.

By crafting a tailored approach that combined explicit vocabulary instruction, strategic text selection, and purposeful vocabulary integration, we were able to create an environment that empowered MLs to access and comprehend complex texts. This success story stands as a testament to the power of collaborative efforts in fostering language and literacy skills, and it reinforces the importance of providing meaningful and structured experiences for MLs to thrive in their educational journeys. This revelation by the teacher was one of the many joys I found when coaching teachers with the ExC-ELL model components.

—Lisa Tartaglia, Assistant Principal and (Former) Coach,
Loudoun County High School

Coaching Vocabulary and Discourse

CHAPTER

#4

From One Coach to Another: Tips for Coaches of Teachers With Multilingual Learners

Coaching teachers is a privilege I don't take lightly. I appreciate it each time a teacher welcomes me into their classroom to watch them teach and to provide feedback. While coaching with the ExC-ELL team, I found it particularly helpful to use the WISEcards they provide that list each component of the ExC-ELL lesson along with a scale to rate the teacher on their use of the component (see an example in Figure 4.9). This guideline kept me focused on the components rather than on the extraneous details I may have noticed that I was not there to judge.

In the end, presenting my commendations and recommendations in a succinct outline was made easy by referring to the WISEcard with my notes. This document was then a useful tool when meeting with the teacher to provide feedback on the use of the strategy I had observed. Both observation documents ensured that the fifteen minutes of observation time and the fifteen minutes of feedback time were sufficient to provide the teachers with a meaningful experience that could positively influence their future teaching practices.

—Cristina Zakis, English for Speakers of Other Languages (ESOL) Coach, Lilburn, Georgia

Vocabulary Across the Disciplines

Coaching with a specific focus on teaching vocabulary and academic language will be the multilingual/multiliteracy coaches' major contribution for all teachers in middle and high schools!

The decision to put the vocabulary chapter after reading does not preclude the importance of teaching vocabulary before students read. Reading comes first in this book because, currently, that is the one area in teaching multilingual learners (MLs) that needs the most attention. Vocabulary has been a widespread axiom since the onset of the COVID-19 pandemic, but it does need revisiting and refining in many schools.

As an ML coach, you will have the wonderful opportunity to work with and inspire educators who may lack sufficient background knowledge and skills to address the diverse linguistic needs of MLs. Teachers will welcome ML coaches who know how to assist with vocabulary instruction for MLs. Now that immigrant student numbers are increasing in every school district, every teacher in the school will need to make some critical changes in their instructional practices. ML coaches will make their shift easier.

Some teachers may not seem eager to learn because they have been asked or told to learn how to work with MLs, and doing so at the beginning stages of these students' English proficiency can be a scary proposition, especially for core content teachers. Yet, once teachers learn a strategy, practice the strategy, see the positive impact it has on their students, and get continuous support from an ML coach, they become avid learners and change agents.

Expert coaches like Elena Aguilar (Bright Morning, 2024) discuss teacher resistance. She recommends we avoid seeing it as resistance but see it for what it really is: fear, confusion, sadness, and sometimes anger. We might not know the teacher's previous experiences with coaching. They might be feeling overwhelmed with too many curriculum innovations. They might be happy with the status quo, feeling they are successful teachers already. They might be struggling with beliefs about MLs or feeling insecure about teaching language and literacy along with their subject area.

MYTH

Coaching vocabulary and academic language might be the major contribution for all middle and high school teachers.

All teachers need recognition for their amazing teaching accomplishments since 2020, despite the COVID-19 interruption. Now, we ask them to make more changes. Society needs to recognize and respect their work under such difficult circumstances—plus schools should offer pay raises, time to learn all these new skills, and a great coach!

So, how do ML coaches of secondary school teachers new to integrating language and content begin to set a positive and flourishing climate for teachers? They follow a sequence and premises for everyone learning and begin by explaining why vocabulary is important.

Why Vocabulary Is Important: What the Research Says

Since the 1980s, there has been an ever-growing body of research on the importance of teaching vocabulary. It evolved in the 1990s and particularly in the 2000s. Here are some important findings from the National Reading Panel (2000) that continue to hold true and can back up your rationale and recommendations for teachers.

From the National Reading Panel

▶ Intentional instruction of vocabulary items is required for all content texts.

▶ Repetition and multiple exposures to vocabulary items are important.

▶ Practicing in rich contexts is valuable for vocabulary learning.

▶ Vocabulary learning should involve active engagement in learning tasks.

▶ Vocabulary tasks should be structured as necessary.

▶ Computer technology can be used effectively to help teach vocabulary.

From the Research Panel on Vocabulary

The seminal book *Teaching and Learning Vocabulary: Bringing Research to Practice* (Hiebert & Kamil, 2005) is a collection of chapters on vocabulary theory, research, and application by major researchers: Nagy, Cunningham, Scott, Stahl, Graves, Hiebert, Kamil, Carlo, August, Beck and McKeown, Biemiller, Calderón, and others. This is a good resource for reading more about the vocabulary instruction that has been the basis of many programs and reading materials. Here are some key messages from the authors:

▶ Command of a large vocabulary frequently sets high-achieving students apart from less successful ones.

▶ The average 6-year-old has a vocabulary of approximately 8,000 words and learns 3,000–5,000 more per year, learning at least 50,000 by high school graduation.

▶ Vocabulary in kindergarten and first grade is a significant predictor of reading comprehension or reading difficulties in the middle and secondary grades.

▶ Vocabulary knowledge correlates with metalinguistic awareness (learning about a language or languages).

▶ Vocabulary knowledge correlates with reading comprehension.

▶ Reading comprehension correlates with procedural and content knowledge.

▶ Content knowledge correlates with academic success.

▶ Comprehension depends on knowing between 90 and 95 percent of the words in a paragraph, on a page, or in a test question.

Not surprisingly, vocabulary development is especially important for MLs. Poor vocabulary is a serious issue for all students. Any student with a small vocabulary bank is less able to comprehend text at grade level (August et al., 2005; Graves et al., 2011). Findings indicate that research-based strategies are effective not only for MLs but for striving readers and all students in general (Calderón et al., 2005).

Teaching and Coaching Language Instruction

Goals for ML Instruction and Coaching

- ✓ Be evidence based and classroom tested.
- ✓ Have a recognizable process for coach, teacher, and students.
- ✓ Use time efficiently.
- ✓ Be highly engaging and effective for everyone's learning.

Principles of Instructional Routines for Academic Language

- ✓ Evidence-based instruction was empirically tested with MLs.
- ✓ Instruction on vocabulary and discourse is explicit.
- ✓ Vocabulary comes from the first- to twelfth-grade classroom texts students are about to read, not lists of words.
- ✓ Student discourse is frequent and deliberately structured in every class.
- ✓ Efficient use of time by teachers and students occurs with more efficient strategies.

Quality implementation begins with the coach and teachers attending together a series of workshops that are orchestrated in a way that makes it easy and practical for teachers to implement vocabulary and discourse instruction. Implementation is easier when key components are presented one at a time at a workshop and the teacher is coached after each workshop.

From Research Into Practice

Multilingual learners are not talking enough!

The three main components of language and literacy learning are *vocabulary/academic language/discourse*, *reading comprehension*, and *writing*. The subcomponents and instructional routines of vocabulary/academic language/discourse instruction can be subdivided into five workshops for teachers and coaches. Workshop facilitators model strategies and participant practice and incorporate them into their lesson at the workshop.

Workshop 1. How to select academically and linguistically demanding vocabulary for MLs in each subject area

- Categories of words
- Types of words for newcomers and other MLs
- Words from texts students are about to read

Workshop 2. How to preteach each word/phrase before students start to read or listen to the information taught in that subject

Workshop 3. How to use those words in oral discourse

Workshop 4. How to assess and integrate vocabulary and oral discourse into lessons (written discourse is approached after reading)

Workshop 5. How to plan lessons, observe vocabulary and discourse in the classrooms, use observation tools, give feedback, and plan with the teacher reasonable, focused, and actionable goals for the next observation

What Coaches Do for Professional Development

 The ML coach requests to attend professional development with the teachers to be coached.

Afterward, the ML coach attends an additional workshop to learn how to use observation protocols, give actionable feedback that increases confidence and motivation, and set a goal for improvement for the teacher.

Expert trainers model the strategies, and teachers and ML coaches practice at the workshops. With help from ML coaches, teachers apply and adapt new learning to their own instructional delivery, as well as to classroom texts, discussions, materials, and lessons. The use of classroom tools for students is part of the training at the workshops. Some of those tools are words, phrases, and sentence frames that students place on their desks or in their folders. These serve as reminders of new words they need to be learning and using in all their subject areas.

Just as coaching helps teachers delve deeper into reading instruction for student mastery, coaching also centers avidly on vocabulary and student talk. The nonevaluative support focuses on increasing efficiency and understanding of MLs' progressions in language proficiency and quality engagement. The teacher–coach knowledge of the vocabulary observation protocol helps them to plan the observation and feedback. The coach knows exactly what a fifteen-minute observation will be about, and the teacher feels comfortable knowing what the coach is looking for in their delivery of explicit vocabulary instruction and student engagement. After receiving valuable feedback, the teacher works with the coach to celebrate and determine the next steps for improving instruction.

The Instructional Model: Selecting Words to Teach

In the Hiebert and Kamil book, Beck and colleagues (2005) present three categories of words—Tiers 1, 2, and 3—in a chapter called "Choosing Words to Teach." Although these categories are very useful for identifying words for all students, Calderón and colleagues (2005) include in their chapter, "Bringing Words to Life in Classrooms With English-Language Learners," other word types that are necessary to select and teach to MLs (see also Gottlieb & Calderón, in press). The three tiers for MLs are listed as follows, with examples.

The Three Tiers Expanded for Multilingual Learners

Tier 3. Subject-specific words that label content from each discipline, concepts, subjects, and topics

Examples: *square root, osmosis, bylaw, photosynthesis, filibuster, polynomial, onomatopoeia, republic, climate change, Shakespeare*

Tier 2. Information-processing words that nest Tier 3 words in long sentences such as polysemous words, transition words, connectors, idioms, cognates, and more sophisticated synonyms for rich discussions and specificity in descriptions

Examples of information-processing words: *due to, effect, affect, forthcoming, generate, implicit, oddly, notwithstanding, point of view, demo, propose, construct, conclude, draw a conclusion, analyze, cite, develop, feature, summarize, distinguish*

Examples of information-processing words that are cognates with Spanish: *elaborate/elaborar, compare/comparar, contrast/contrastar, describe/describir, details/detalles, determine/determinar, evaluate/evaluar, evidence/evidencia, interpret/interpretar, persuade/persuadir, infer/inferir, inference/inferencia, assume/asumir, relevant/relevante, structure/estructura, demonstrate/demostrar*

Examples of sophisticated words for rich discussions and specificity in descriptions (instead of always using simple words like *say*, MLs can learn to use these instead): *express, denote, ascertain, promote, pontificate, reiterate, whisper, scream, announce, request, reveal* (see also "Specificity in Lieu of *Say*" on pages 129–130)

Examples of transition or connecting words: *initially, subsequently, nevertheless, however, therefore, so that, moreover, for instance, notwithstanding, thus*

Examples of polysemous (multiple-meaning) words and idioms: *power, cell, right, left, face, radical, check, trunk, bank, leg, break a leg, shake a leg, no leg to stand on, hand, hand me the book, hand-me-down, round, state, table, fall*

Examples of homophones (words that sound the same but are spelled differently and have different meanings): *there/their/ they're, by/buy/bye, cell/sell/sail, four/for, sun/son, see/sea, flour/flower, knight/night*

Examples of heteronyms (words where different pronunciation = different meaning): *desert* (geographic region or the act of leaving); *wind* (weather or the act of turning something)

Tier 1. Basic words MLs need to communicate, read, and write. These words may be difficult to pronounce, spell, or figure out the meaning from pictures because of lack of exposure to items or common idioms. However, throughout the day, MLs use social language to communicate with peers and educators to build relationships or express personal issues and needs. Those seemingly easy words are sometimes called Tier 1. They seem easy to us but some MLs never had opportunities to learn them. In essence, Tiers 1, 2, and 3 are requisite for all MLs to access core content mastery.

Examples: *they're, their, there;* idioms such as *hang in there, dance around the topic, spit it out, shake a leg*

Source: Adapted from Gottlieb and Calderón (in press).

Vocabulary knowledge is part of what enables us to know which pronunciation is correct and monitor whether the text with that word makes sense. The links among phonology, orthography, and words' meanings (i.e., vocabulary) are at the heart of orthographic mapping: the linking of words' spellings, pronunciations, and meanings in memory (Ehri, 2014), which is so much more important for second-language learners (Calderón, 2007).

The Complexity of Polysemous Words

Polysemous words are particularly troublesome for second-language learners. The multiple meanings of these words can easily confuse a student. For example, a mathematics teacher has just taught about the "power" of a number as an exponent. Afterward, a science teacher talks about hydrogen "power." Subsequently, in government class, the teacher discusses executive "power," and students are thinking about how the word *power* fits in all these classes. Unless each teacher presents the meaning and background connections of the word as it is to be used in context in that class, it will be very difficult for an ML to keep up. A student might see the word *wind*, but if they don't know 90 percent of the words around it, they won't know how to pronounce it ("Let's wind down"; "When the White House officials get wind of the plan, they immediately wind up running out into the cold windy night").

At first glance, some polysemous words appear to be Tier 1 because they seem so easy (*face, right, left, hand, table, wind*), but take a look in Figure 4.1 at the word *table* and the way it can be used across different subject areas or in conversations.

Figure 4.1   Example of a Polysemous Word

**Polysemous Words:
How many different ways do we use *table*?**

dinner table   coffee table

under the table   **table**   water table

on the table/
off the table   table of contents

"Let's table this   "Find the value of *x*
discussion."   on the table."

Source: © 2023 Margarita Calderón & Associates. www.ExC-ELL.com

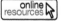 Available for download at http://resources.corwin.com/CMLExcellence

An Activity for You

Select one polysemous word, phrase, or idiom and list all the ways students might encounter it:

▶ Across all subjects

▶ In movies

▶ In the news

▶ At home

Cross-Linguistic Supports
The Benefits of Using Cognates and Translanguaging

Teachers and coaches must understand that they can and should build cross-linguistic connections (i.e. applying what is learned in one language to situations presented in another language) between their home language and English to encourage skill transfer and develop metalinguistic awareness (i.e., understanding of how language works and can be used to learn the second language).

Cognates

Diane August and her colleagues (Artzi et al., 2019; August et al., 2005; August et al., 2023) suggest several strategies that appear to be especially valuable for building the vocabularies of MLs in science and mathematics. These strategies include taking advantage of students' first language if the language shares cognates with English, teaching the meaning of basic words, and providing sufficient review and reinforcement. Because English and Spanish share many cognate pairs, this instructional strategy is especially useful for Spanish-speaking MLs (see Figure 4.2). Spanish-speaking students can draw on their cognate knowledge as a means of figuring out unfamiliar words in English. This is an obvious bridge to the English language if the student is made aware of how to use this resource.

Even if teachers and coaches don't know Spanish, they can Google the word and ask for the cognate. Students can do this, too. Teachers should encourage students to be aware of similarities in spelling. Looking at spelling differences actually teaches students to be good spellers in English. Other languages that have Greek or Latin roots like Italian, French, and Portuguese have cognates with English as well.

Figure 4.2   Examples of Cognates Between Spanish and English

hypothesis	hipótesis
observation	observación
classification	clasificación
prediction	predicción
tentative conclusion	conclusión tentativa
evaluate	evaluar
experiment	experimento
investigation	investigación

Translanguaging

Translanguaging is an emerging construct in second-language learning (Seals, 2021) that appears to have several benefits. Empirical studies are still emerging, but there are enough qualitative studies that promote classroom application. The purpose of translanguaging is for students to use their first language alongside English as a tool for learning a concept. Sometimes there is too much translation in all grade levels. MLs become highly dependent on translation from the teacher, peers, or devices. Translanguaging offers an opportunity for emergent bilinguals to display their understanding of content-area material when they are permitted to use it in class. Students are not restricted to responding in only one language. This builds self-confidence in speaking and increases success in building vocabulary and reading comprehension (Dougherty, 2021). Most importantly, it shows that we value their home language when we give them time and permission to use it in class with peers. Translanguaging is a common fifth register for bilinguals. A fifth register, as seen in Figure 4.3, is a register that can occur in any language or any language register we choose.

ML coaches can help teachers maximize this capital to help advance academic growth and progress. For example, students use their first language to read about a topic in history, literature, mathematics, or science. They write about it in their primary language and later discuss it in English with peers to clarify concepts or process. Afterward, they work together to formally paraphrase into English. This is followed by discussions and more reading and writing in English. Languages can work together in the classroom when teachers plan strategically to pair students so they can negotiate meaning and explore together, thereby building their proficiency in both languages (Calderón et al., 2019; Gottlieb & Calderón, in press).

Caveat. Students must also understand that the primary goal is to become fully bilingual, which means that their English must become as proficient as their Spanish or other home language. Both languages should continue to develop to become bilingual and biliterate. Therefore, once they have discussed information with same-language peers using translanguaging, they must summarize or answer questions as much as possible in English. The onus is on the students to learn academic English as quickly as possible to balance their bilingual proficiencies.

Figure 4.3   Different Discourses

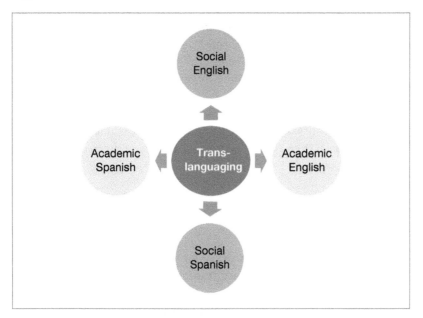

An Activity for You

Reflect on all the aspects of language that have been presented so far. What are some of your thoughts, insights, and implications for teachers and yourself as a coach?

NEW INSIGHT SO FAR	IMPLICATIONS FOR TEACHERS	IMPLICATIONS FOR COACHES

Tier 2 Information-Processing Words Found in State Exams

The following words come from the first four pages of the Virginia sixth-grade science state exam: *absence, accuracy, additive, affect, allow, analogous, apparent, approach, arrange, assortment, assumption, basis, bases, behavior, belief, body, boundary, coincide, compiled, core, criteria, crucial, denote, depict, deplete, device, display, distinct, due to, effect, forthcoming, generate, illustrate, impact, implicit, notwithstanding, oddly, so that, solely, successive, state, underlying, vary, whereby,* and *widespread*. These are not common everyday words, and they are often among the words that trip up MLs in their state exams.

   Caveat. Please don't teach these words as a list. Lists of words taught out of context will be forgotten by the next day. Keep this list handy and teach the words in context when they occur in a text the students are about to read.

Tier 2 Words for Connecting Discourse or Making Transitions

When discussing a text's structures or an author's intent, there are words that help connect thoughts and expression of feelings or that facilitate the transition to another topic. Once these words are practiced verbally in discussions, the students will automatically use them in writing.

> ▪ **Cause and effect:** *because, due to, as a result, since, for this reason, therefore, in order to, so that, thus,* and so on

> ▪ **Contrast:** *or, but, although, however, in contrast, nevertheless, on the other hand, while,* and so on

> ▪ **Addition or comparison:** *and, also, as well as, in addition, likewise, moreover, by the way,* and so on

> ▪ **Giving examples:** *for example, for instance, in particular, such as,* and so on

Sophisticated Words for Specificity

Students need to continuously learn more words for specificity. These come in handy when describing characters in a novel, sequences in engineering, or a science experiment. Learning words for specificity also helps students avoid repeating the same words such as *and* or *say*. Instead of *say*, words such as *comment* sound more sophisticated, or words like *converse* might be more appropriate in a specific context. Many of those "fancy" words are also cognates. Here are some examples.

SPECIFICITY IN LIEU OF *SAY*	
converse	conversar
specify	especificar
comment	comentar
mention	mencionar
verbalize	verbalizar
articulate	articular

Practitioners must be presented with a model of reading that names vocabulary and makes clear that vocabulary knowledge may be affecting not only students' language comprehension but also their word recognition (Duke et al., 2021), and this is key for second-language learners (Calderón & Tartaglia, 2023).

What Coaches Do to Assist Teachers

Multilingual coaches help teachers select words to teach every day in every subject. There are criteria for selecting words to teach before reading or discussing. First, the text needs to be chunked and parsed for focus and manageability and analyzed for words MLs might need to learn to comprehend the text. One page at a time might suffice to begin this practice.

From that page, teachers will need help in selecting the words that will be most useful for comprehension. An ML coach can assist by first finding the Tier 3 words in a text. Tier 3 words are easy to find because they are usually highlighted in bold, are in the glossary, and are recognizable as specific to the topic. Once the Tier 3 words are found, they are set aside. These words will be learned in the context of reading since the text typically defines them in sentences or will have pictures and graphics.

Coaches may also help by selecting Tier 2 words instead. The key is to find Tier 2 words and phrases that nest Tier 3 words in long sentences or that help students to understand Tier 3 words. A teacher will most likely find "a lot of words" and will need help to narrow those lists down to five or six words. For example, the following sentence is full of Tier 2 words about climate but doesn't even mention the Tier 3 word *climate*: "Some communities experience disproportionate impacts because of existing vulnerabilities, historical patterns of inequity, socioeconomic disparities, and systemic environmental injustices (i.e., redlining)" (Environmental Protection Agency [EPA], 2024). Here are some tips for helping teachers select words to preteach (see also Figures 4.4 and 4.5).

Figure 4.4 Criteria for Selecting Words to Preteach

✓ **The word/phrase is critical to the understanding of the concept.**
✓ **It will probably appear on a test.**
✓ **It is critically important to the discipline.**
✓ **It is critically important to this unit.**
✓ **You want to hear it in students' partner summaries.**
✓ **You want to see it in their exit pass (a quick-write at the end of class to summarize what they learned in class) or in a writing assignment.**

 Available for download at http://resources.corwin.com/CMLExcellence

Select words from the text students are about to read, such as one of the following types, that they will need to learn in order to comprehend the text:

▶ Chapter in a textbook (social studies)

▶ Word problem (mathematics)

▶ Lab directions (science)

▶ Poem (English language arts)

▶ Written definition of a Tier 3 word

▶ Written script of a song or play

▶ Video clip

▶ Lecture

▶ Newspaper article

▶ Cooking directions

▶ Internet pages

Also look for Tier 1 words and phrases that need to be taught to newcomers before watching a video, reading an online text, or engaging in classroom procedures:

▶ Asking for classroom materials (names of classroom materials)

▶ Asking for explanations or clarification

▶ Using the computer (parts of the computer, how to start the computer, easy-word instructions)

▶ Using polite discourse (*excuse me, I'm sorry, thanks, please*)

▶ Using sentence starters (*I agree with Linda and want to add _____.*)

▶ Using sentence frames (*_____ has had a big effect on my life because _____.*)

Figure 4.5 What to Look For in the Teacher's Text

- Types of sentences (simple, compound, complex)
- Connotations, double meanings, ambiguity, metaphors, similes, idioms, associations, analogies
- Cognates, false cognates, Latin roots, affixes
- Polysemous words, homophones
- Active and passive voice
- Word categories (Tiers 1, 2, and 3)
- Spelling patterns, phonemes, morphemes
- Word order and collocations (blue dress; the flag is red, white, and blue)
- Antonyms, synonyms, rhyming words

online resources Available for download at http://resources.corwin.com/CMLExcellence

Reasons to Select Words as a Precursor to Comprehension

A text that is read becomes a mentor text because it serves as a model for sentence structures and later for text-based writing.

A text becomes all of the following:

▶ The source of vocabulary for preteaching before reading or conversations

▶ An exemplar for grammar, writing function or structure, and/or language usage

▶ The focus of reading, summarizing, and writing to meet standards/objectives

▶ The focus for development of metacognitive and social-emotional skills

Activities for You

1. How would you explain (in an "elevator speech," or brief pitch) the three tiers to a new teacher who wasn't able to attend the workshop?

2. Practice selecting Tier 3 words from the following text, "Climate Equity." Highlight them using a color such as the examples in the first paragraph that are set in **bold**.

3. Use a different color to practice selecting Tier 2 words from "Climate Equity." See examples of Tier 2 words in the first paragraph that are underlined.

Climate Equity

Climate change does not affect all people equally. Some communities experience disproportionate impacts because of existing vulnerabilities, historical patterns of inequity, socioeconomic disparities, and systemic environmental injustices (e.g., redlining). People who already face the greatest burdens are often the ones affected most by climate change.

EPA is committed to supporting communities—particularly those facing disproportionate impacts—develop and implement equitable solutions to climate change impacts. Only through collaboration across all communities and levels of government can the nation make progress in addressing systemic factors that impact climate equity.

Climate equity is the goal of recognizing and addressing the unequal burdens made worse by climate change, while ensuring that all people share the benefits of climate protection efforts. Achieving equity means that all people—regardless of their race, color, gender, age, sexuality, national origin, ability, or income—live in safe, healthy, fair communities.

Source: Environmental Protection Agency. (2024, January 2). Climate change impacts: Climate equity. https://www.epa.gov/climateimpacts/climate-equity

Vignette: Categorizing Words

*Ms. Medrano prefers to use a graphic organizer such as Figure 4.6.
She wants to anticipate which polysemous words or idioms
in "Climate Equity" (EPA, 2024) she might have to preteach.
Her coach has informed her that there are different ways of
categorizing Tier 2 and 3 words. There is no absolute right answer.
The important thing is to see which words her MLs/striving
readers might not be familiar with and thus she should preteach.*

Figure 4.6   Chart for Identifying and Classifying Words to Teach
(With Example Words From "Climate Equity")

TYPE	TIER 3	TIER 2	TIER 1
Polysemous words		*face, change*	
Cognates	*climate, socioeconomic, communities, systemic*	*affect, inequality, equally, affected, experience, impact, existing, vulnerability, injustice*	
Idioms			
Connectors or transition words			*because of*
Homophones			*already*
Others	*redlining*		

*Although Ms. Medrano feels that more could be added, she opts
for focusing on Tier 2 words. The students will need to read
to learn the Tier 3 words, and since her MLs are proficienct at
Levels 3 and 4 (see Chapter 2, Figure 2.2, for examples of English
language proficiency levels), they will not be needing any Tier 1
words from this passage. She thanks her coach for helping her
identify these words and for confirming she is on the right track.
She invites the coach to come and observe her teach five of those
words the next day.*

An Activity for You

1. Parse an upcoming passage from any text such as a newspaper article that you can use as your mentor text.

2. Use a chart such as Figure 4.6 to choose five words from the text to preteach.

3. For K–2 students or newcomers, choose Tier 1 words as well.

4. After your practice, help a teacher select words from a classroom text.

Preteaching Five Words Before Students Read

Once the five or six words or phrases have been selected, a seven-step strategy can be used for preteaching vocabulary to the whole class (see Figure 4.7). Non-MLs benefit from the clarity of meaning, better pronunciation, and practice of academic discourse. In the ExC-ELL study in New York City and Kauai, Hawaii, by Calderón (2007), the seven steps were tested and refined until teachers and students found them effective. When compared to other five- or six-step strategies being used, MLs using the seven steps outperformed those using other models, as evidenced by the Woodcock-Muñoz vocabulary battery ($d = 1.10$).

Figure 4.7 Preteaching Words/Phrases With the Seven-Step Approach

1. The teacher asks students to repeat the word/phrase three times. This is to practice pronunciation.

2. The teacher states the word/phrase in context using the sentence in the text. It will help MLs remember the meaning when they read that part of the text.

3. The teacher provides the dictionary definition of the word/phrase. Students will take too long to look it up in the dictionary. If it's a polysemous word, they won't know which meaning to select.

4. The teacher provides a student-friendly definition or an example of the word/phrase. This helps anchor the correct meaning.

5. The teacher highlights features of the word/phrase (spelling, polysemous, cognate, tense, prefix, etc.). This helps MLs to become exposed to grammar.

6. The students engage in discourse for 60 seconds using a teacher-provided sentence starter or sentence frame. Partners take turns giving an example in complete sentences. In 60 seconds, each can give four or five examples that use the word/phrase.

7. The teacher informs students when they will use the word/phrase (e.g., in verbal summaries, writing assignments, projects).

The seven steps are used with MLs and the whole class. All students need to learn more vocabulary.

Efficiency is a must. Each word or phrase should only take two minutes to teach (ten minutes total for five words). Students need time for reading and learning the content. The teacher has one minute to deliver Steps 1 to 5, and students practice for one minute sharing four or five examples, each using the sentence frame. Step 7 only takes a few seconds. It is the accountability step where students are informed when they will be monitored or expected to use the word or phrase. Compared to other vocabulary strategies such as the Frayer model, where students are asked to copy the definition of the word, write a sentence with the word, or draw a picture that illustrates the word. Students spend ten or more minutes with only one word, copying, writing, and not using it verbally. In comparison, the seven-step strategy expedites the learning of five words in ten minutes, including five minutes of verbal practice in their own sentences.

Step 6 is the most important because this is where partners practice using the word aloud with their own examples in complete sentences. The non-MLs learn just as much when paired with an ML. They also get to practice social-emotional competencies.

Sentence frames must be carefully constructed to enable several examples from each partner. The sentence frame must include the target word or phrase so the students can say it in each example. Some words will require background knowledge for students to give five examples. The teachers will need to rehearse with the sentence frame they create to make sure that students can give four or five examples, each from their background knowledge.

Vignette: Preteaching With the Seven Steps

Ms. Moore has invited her coach to observe her teach the seven steps for the first time. She wants the coach to observe her do Steps 1 to 5 and to walk around the room and listen to the partners as they practice using the selected word in Step 6. She writes the steps on a PowerPoint.

(Continued)

(Continued)

1. Say *subsequently* three times.

2. *Subsequently, we prepare the main ingredients in the formula.*

3. The dictionary says it means *afterwards*, *thereafter*, or *eventually*.

4. It basically means *later* or *next*.

5. It is a cognate with Spanish: *subsecuentemente*. Notice the endings of both words.

6. Use this frame to ping-pong back and forth for one minute and give five or six examples each.

   I got up early this morning, and subsequently I _____.

7. Use *subsequently* in your verbal summaries during your partner reading, plus in today's exit pass.

Teacher and Coach Reflection

When the coach asks Ms. Moore how she feels about her lesson, she replies, "I'm disappointed because only some of my students gave me examples for Step 6. The multilingual partners weren't even trying. Was it a bad sentence frame? What do you think went wrong?" The coach began by telling her that her Steps 1 to 5 were well delivered and the frame for Step 6 worked well with the three students who raised their hands when she asked for examples. The coach then shows her the playbook, which says that Step 6 is for partners to come up with five or six examples each for one minute. Ms. Moore immediately realizes that instead of giving the class one minute for partner talk, she asked for individual student answers. The same three students who always answer were the only ones who raised their hands. She says, "I am so used to asking questions to the class, to whoever wants to answer. I need to give students time to talk with their partners where they feel more comfortable practicing their new words. Can you come back tomorrow and let me try this again? Seeing you will remind me not to change that Step 6." The coach agrees to return and says she will bring a sheet of paper with "Step 6" written in large letters to hold up when Ms. Moore gets to Step 6. They both laugh and agree it is good to have a backup reminder.

What Coaches Do: The Coaching Protocol for Vocabulary

You can use the checklists in Figures 4.8, 4.9, and 4.10 or construct one of your own for observations and feedback on the seven steps or whatever steps your school is using to teach a word or phrase. Make sure that your process and your observation tool are consistent across all instructional contexts. Is the protocol working with MLs across the subjects? Are all the teachers using it, and do they find it valuable? Do you? When it is time to analyze and report the data for the whole school, does it fit nicely into patterns? The protocols outlined in Figures 4.8 and 4.9 have been tested in multiple settings and continue to be used for data gathering and for feedback.

Is the observation protocol giving you good data about MLs' vocabulary progression across the disciplines?

Be sure to share your protocol with the teacher when you give feedback. Showing the data makes it easier on the coach and the conversation. Here are two examples (see Figures 4.8 and 4.9).

Figure 4.8 Coaching Protocol for the Vocabulary Seven Steps

VOCABULARY WORDS INTRODUCED IN THIS LESSON:				
1.	2.	3.	4.	5.

Name of teacher: _____   Subject: _____   Date: _____

LOOK FOR:	COMMENTS:
There is 100% engagement by students during vocabulary instruction.	
Steps 1–5 take one minute or less, and all five steps are presented.	

(Continued)

(Continued)

LOOK FOR:	COMMENTS:
Teacher supplies a sentence frame for Step 6 that contains the target word/phrase.	
The sentence frame is effectively used by MLs and all students. The frame reinforces the meaning of the word/phrase and allows students to complete it with their own background knowledge.	
Students engage with the seven steps orally, without writing or drawing.	
Students are held accountable for using the word/phrase later in reading and writing activities.	

Successes to celebrate (student or teacher, big or small):

Additional comments:

Source: © ExC-ELL Observation Protocol, Margarita Calderón & Associates.

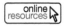 Available for download at http://resources.corwin.com/CMLExcellence

When teachers want to see information on the students' performance, a second type of protocol is preferred because the ML coach can use seating charts to keep track of student performance. The teacher can have a chart ready, or the ML coach can draw the seating arrangement. A tool such as Figure 4.9 can be used to tabulate by using various indicators to represent students who are highly engaged but struggling, disengaged, or moving quickly and ready for a bigger challenge.

Figure 4.9 ExC-ELL Observation Protocol (EOP) for the Vocabulary Seven Steps

Walk-Through of Instructional Strategies With ExC-ELL (EOP WISEcard™)

Teacher _____ **Grade:** _____ **Subject:** _____ **Date:** _____ **Observer:** _____

Materials: _____

Class size: _____ # OF ELs _____ # OF SPED/ELs _____

Teacher Posts and Explains:

Content Objective/Standard: _____

Language Objective: _____

Essential Question: _____

Theme/Topic: _____

Tiered Vocab Chart: ☐ Yes ☐ No ☐ All 3 ☐ Partial: ☐ T1 ☐ T2 ☐ T3

Connectors/Sentence Starters Chart(s) ☐ Connectors ☐ Starters ☐ None

VOCABULARY & ORACY	1–4
1 = Emerging 2 = Developing 3 = Effective 4 = Highly Effective	✓

Tier 1 _____ Tier 2 _____

Tier 3 _____ Comment:

V1 Teacher asks students to repeat the word.

V2 Teacher states the word in context from the text.

V3 Teacher provides the dictionary/glossary definition.

V4 Teacher provides a student-friendly definition.

V5 Teacher highlights features: polysemous, cognate, tense, prefixes, etc.

V6 Teacher engages 100% of the students in using the word verbally with their partner. Students engage in teacher-provided sentence starter or frame for 60 seconds (must contain target vocab.) four or five times each.

V7 Teacher informs when students will see and use it.

Comments:

Class Set-up

The Instructional Model: Setting Up a Context for Social-Emotional Learning

Like the application of social-emotional competencies for reading, the students are asked to practice word learning with a peer in a timely fashion, with effort, and on their best behavior. Vocabulary practice is where *social-emotional learning (SEL) competencies* such as self-awareness and self-management can be practiced.

Figure 4.10 summarizes the five key competencies and how they relate to learning vocabulary as previously identified by Calderón and Tartaglia (2023).

Figure 4.10   Social-Emotional Learning for Vocabulary

COMPETENCY	WHAT IT IS	HOW IT RELATES TO LEARNING VOCABULARY
Self-awareness	The ability to understand one's emotions, thoughts, and values that influence behavior across situations	For Step 1 of vocabulary preteaching, they must pronounce the word/phrase three times without hesitation in sync with the rest of the class. Older students might be embarrassed at first and have to realize why it is important. For Step 6, each partner must be aware of their own feelings about talking with another student and portray the right attitude. They must be willing to practice speaking with a peer for a whole minute.
Self-management	The ability to understand one's emotions to achieve one's goals and aspirations	For Step 6, each partner must control their feelings and focus on accomplishing the turn-taking as they share four or five examples for a whole minute. They must keep in mind that the main task is mastery of the word/phrase they are practicing with a peer.
Social awareness	The ability to understand and empathize with others, especially those from diverse social and cultural backgrounds, English proficiencies, and emotional states	During Step 6, partners show respect for one another, use positive talk, and do not get distracted.
Relationship skills	The ability to establish and maintain healthy and supportive relationships and to effectively navigate settings with diverse individuals and groups	During Step 6, partners must be open to creating a relationship of trust, respect, and friendly communication with whatever partner they have been assigned.

COMPETENCY	WHAT IT IS	HOW IT RELATES TO LEARNING VOCABULARY
Responsible decision making	The ability to make caring and constructive choices about personal behavior and social interactions across settings.	During all vocabulary steps, students remain engaged, repeat the word/phrase three times, actively listen to Steps 2 to 5, practice Step 6 with a peer, put their working memory to work to retain all new knowledge, and use that knowledge as the teacher requires during Step 7.

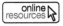 Available for download at http://resources.corwin.com/CMLExcellence

Once students know what is expected of them in a vocabulary task, they often learn rapidly (Hiebert & Kamil, 2005). The seven steps become much more efficient and effective routines when the majority of teachers are using the seven steps and the five SEL competencies. The ML coach can also use the seven steps to help the teacher plan, observe, listen to, and record the students. With all these preparations and routines, students quickly become comfortable and look forward to learning vocabulary in this fashion.

An Activity for You

Reflect on all the aspects of social-emotional learning that have been presented so far. What are some of your thoughts, insights, and implications for teachers and yourself as a coach?

NEW INSIGHT ON SEL	IMPLICATIONS FOR TEACHERS	IMPLICATIONS FOR COACHES

An Instructional Model for Discourse

Multilingual learners need to talk more!

Discourse is written or verbal communication. The larger the vocabulary, the stronger the communication. A strong working oral vocabulary is the basis of reading comprehension and quality writing. Students who work in pairs, triads, and teams have an opportunity to learn how to use new words in sentences and strings of sentences in discourse. Discourse can be practiced as a whole class and in teacher-to-student, student-to-student, and parent/family-to-child moments. All are great opportunities to practice and learn new words and patterns.

Three Dimensions to Be Explicitly Taught

1. The word/phrase dimension employs meanings for communication across all subjects.

2. The sentence dimension contributes to the grammatical complexity of a text or oral discourse. Students need to know and use various sentence types.

3. The discourse dimension is overall meaning across an entire text and how the user constructs a meaningful message (Moats, 2020; WIDA, 2020).

Discourse patterns are built around words and phrases that MLs need for different purposes beyond describing content. They need scaffolding with sentence frames or sentence starters to practice effective communication during cooperative learning; science, technology, engineering, and mathematics (STEM); or project-based learning activities.

Speaking and Listening as Formative Assessment

Student discourse can be used for formative assessment of vocabulary. How many new words is the student using this week in discourse? Are those words used accurately? Can the student speak in strings of discourse beyond one-phrase answers?

To create a comfort zone for practicing discourse, teachers can distribute word cards or table tents before an activity. For example, cards such as Figure 4.11 can contain SEL competencies, phrases, and sentence starters MLs will need for discussions.

Figure 4.11   Team Talk

☐ **Politely disagree.**

☐ **Elaborate on an idea.**

☐ **Interrupt or ask for a turn.**

☐ **Offer an opinion.**

☐ **Offer a suggestion.**

☐ **Ask for help.**

☐ **Offer help.**

All content teachers want to be purposeful with student interaction. When MLs are not talking enough, they may be afraid to make mistakes, particularly the long-term English learners who have been burned many times in many classrooms. ML coaches can help them establish a classroom climate where no one is afraid to make mistakes when talking. Posting the SEL competencies or the social norms of interaction, as shown in Figure 4.12, reminds all students about the behaviors that are expected in the classroom.

Figure 4.12   Norms for Peer Interaction

✓ **Be kind.**

✓ **Listen to your partner.**

✓ **Help your partner but don't give answers.**

✓ **Take turns.**

There will be behaviors that emerge now and then, and the teacher can add to this list or change them as necessary. Regardless, it is good to change the wording often. *Kind* can become *considerate*, and *help* can be switched to *assist* or *support*.

Encourage teachers to encourage MLs to speak in class as much as possible. Conversations can be structured around books and subjects that build vocabulary. Instead of simple "yes or no" questions, ask questions that are interactive and meaningful. Have MLs discuss them with a buddy before they answer in class. For example, "What do you think? What should we change?" With such opportunities to talk, MLs will learn the academic English necessary to succeed in that subject area. But first, let them talk it out and prepare what they want to say.

Teacher beliefs and low expectations have been hindering MLs for decades. Rigorous instruction with support will begin to change those low expectations because MLs will live up to the expectations. Students will welcome opportunities to talk after they are explicitly taught to interact with peers and given some discourse prompts (see Figure 4.13).

Figure 4.13   Checklist for Coaches Helping Teachers to Teach Discourse

- ☐ Interacting with peers during virtual or in-person class discussions (turn-taking, polite interruptions, agreeing or disagreeing, restating, concluding).

- ☐ Interacting with a buddy to practice vocabulary, listening, verbal discourse, partner reading, verbal summarization, or paired writing.

- ☐ Summarizing the teacher's instructions, facts being presented, or a small chunk of text just read.

- ☐ Working with teams during team projects, team writing, or team performances.

- ☐ Cooperating, helping, accepting help, expressing own views, suspending own views, accepting others' views, and other social protocols that the learning might require.

- ☐ Using translanguaging as a resource to clarify meaning but additionally working with peers to provide responses in English.

online resources   Available for download at http://resources.corwin.com/CMLExcellence

Without explicit instruction of words, phrases, or sentences, MLs become self-conscious and afraid, and fail to interact with their peers. Peer relationships are an essential part of a healthy development. Without relationships, students can develop a sense of isolation leading to absenteeism and other undesirable behaviors.

After students read, enact the use of the vocabulary to make sense of the text and ask questions that guide them to think about the word meanings in a comprehension-centric fashion. Chapter 3 on reading gives practical examples of discourse. Teachers, not just ML coaches, must make notations of the students' discourse for formative assessment. In summary, coaches help to integrate vocabulary, reading, and writing with discourse in all content areas (see Figure 4.14).

Figure 4.14 Coaches Help to Integrate Language, Literacy, Content and Coaching Cycles

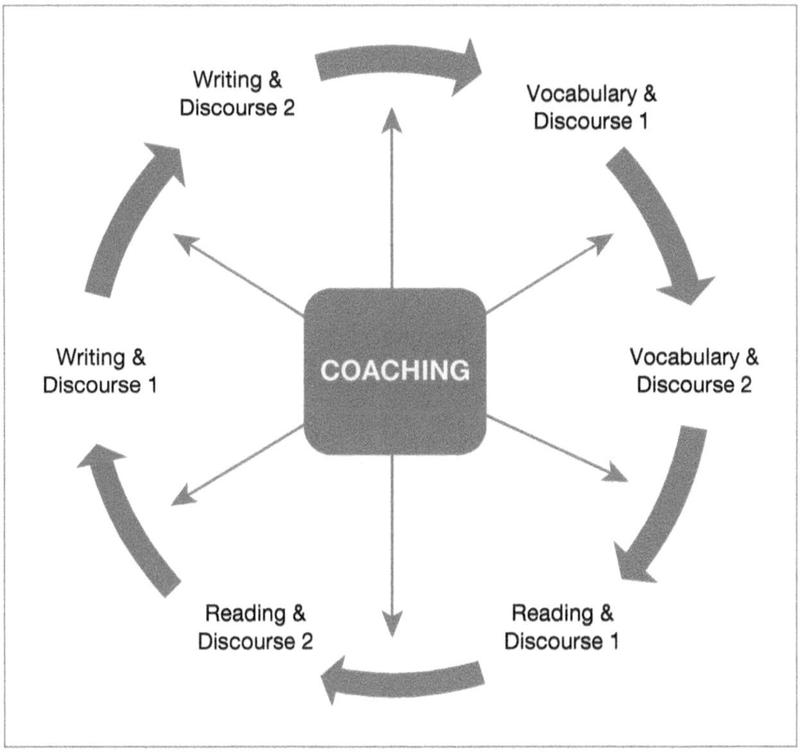

Social-Emotional Learning Discourse

If we want students to learn and apply SEL competencies, they need to practice using key words/phrases with peers during any partner or team activity. SEL-specific vocabulary comes in handy during visits with counselors and class meetings. The internet has graphics for checking on students' feelings that can be used to teach vocabulary. Using a chart such as Figure 4.15, a teacher can select one word from each category to teach daily. Useful words such as these can be taught "on the run"—that is, immediately when they are needed. Use Step 1 to ensure pronunciation, Step 4 to give an example of the word's meaning, and Step 6 for one or two examples of the word in full sentences from the student.

Figure 4.15   Example of Words to Preteach for SEL Activities

HAPPY	SAD	SURPRISED	FEARFUL	DISAPPOINTED	ANGRY
Playful	Lonely	Startled	Scared	Frustrated	Enraged
Proud	Discouraged	Confused	Nervous	Let down	Livid
Accepted	Hurt	Energized	Worried	Shocked	Troubled
Creative	Embarrassed	Exhilarated	Tense	Anxious	Fuming

An Activity for You

Reflect on all the aspects of interaction that have been presented so far. What are some of your thoughts, insights, and implications for teachers and yourself as a coach?

NEW INSIGHT ON INTERACTION	IMPLICATIONS FOR TEACHERS	IMPLICATIONS FOR COACHES

What Coaches Do: Coaching Protocol for Discourse

A checklist can be used for collecting information in a practical and very visual way. The observation protocol in Figure 4.16, just as the others in this book, collects information as objectively as possible. It is also in a format that can be shown to the teacher before the observation to plan and afterward during the feedback, debriefing, and reflection stage. If additional context is necessary for observing the discourse activity, the top of the checklist will help to collect that information. Otherwise, a coach can use the bottom only.

Coaches and teachers have the option of using a numeric value of 1 to 4 (1 = *Emerging*, 2 = *Developing*, 3 = *Effective*, 4 = *Highly Effective*) or using a check mark to indicate that the event took place.

Figure 4.16 Observation Protocol for Discourse/Interaction

Teacher: _____ Date: _____

Content Objective/Standard: _____

Language Objective: _____

Essential Question: _____

Theme/Topic: _____

Connectors/Sentence Starters Chart(s): _____

_____

VOCABULARY & DISCOURSE 1 = EMERGING 2 = DEVELOPING 3 = EFFECTIVE 4 = HIGHLY EFFECTIVE	1–4 ✓
Discourse pattern or sentence frame: _____ _____ _____	
D1 Teacher preteaches a discourse pattern(s) using the 7 steps.	
D2 Teacher states the objective of the topic to be discussed.	
D3 Teacher provides table tents with key phrases/patterns.	
D4 Teacher engages 100% of the students in using the pattern(s) verbally with their partner. Students engage in interaction with teacher-provided sentence starter or frame for 60 seconds (must contain target vocab.) four or five times each.	
D5 Teacher monitors to record accuracy or areas that need further instruction.	
D6 Teacher debriefs/discusses with whole class to anchor concepts and assess verbal discourse.	
Comments:	

Source: ©ExC-ELL Observation Protocol, Margarita Calderón & Associates.

Teaching English for Academic Purposes: Language Functions

Proficiency in a language for academic purposes requires that students be competent at performing sophisticated "language functions" used in rich discussions or further study of a topic. For such, MLs must be prepared to do all of the following:

▶ Argue persuasively for or against a point of view.

▶ Analyze, compare, and contrast.

▶ Evaluate alternative points of view and factual information.

▶ Justify one's point of view or debate different points of view.

▶ Synthesize and integrate information.

▶ Follow or give complex directions.

▶ Hypothesize about the causal relationship between events.

▶ Justify a predication, as in a science experiment on osmosis.

▶ Present a logical argument.

▶ Question an explanation.

What Coaches Do to Emphasize Academic Language

ML coaches can remind teachers that academic language differs from one subject to another; for example, the language of mathematics is different from the language used to discuss and write about science and history. The language of different academic subjects can differ in multiple ways. Each subject requires knowledge of specific technical vocabulary. This means that students must learn alternative meanings of common words, such as the example given in Figure 4.1 for the word *table*.

Academic language also differs from subject to subject concerning grammatical forms and discourse patterns that are typically used when talking or writing about these subjects. For example, science might call for grammatical skills that allow students to formulate hypotheses using subjunctive verb forms and to express relationships in probabilistic terms (e.g., "if the boats were heavier, then they would probably sink") or to express causal relationships (e.g., "humidity is a function of both temperature and proximity to large bodies of water"), but mathematics might call on these grammatical forms and discourse functions much less often.

Studies by Umansky and Reardon (2014) and Carhill and colleagues (2008) indicate further that understanding the development of proficiency in English among MLs requires a multidimensional, longitudinal approach since development is not linear but fluctuates over grades and is influenced by multiple factors.

Benefits and Pitfalls of Technology

Technology can be a powerful tool for newcomers and MLs who need translations, to hear their voices and pronunciation, or to revisit video recordings. There are technologies to help them understand text or a teacher's directions. There is an earbud translation tool (WT2 Edge Translator Earbuds), along with online translation tools and other emerging tools. Most textbooks that are online also have a translation tool.

Caveats. One thing to watch for is the relevancy of the translations. Irrelevant translations occur frequently with polysemous words. For example, *éxito* may be translated as *exit* instead of *success*; *in effect* may be translated as *en efectivo*, which means "in cash." If a student looks up *Add it to the table*, it will give *Agrégalo a la mesa* (dining table).

Another thing to gauge is how dependent the MLs are becoming on translations. Translations are occasionally beneficial tools for the comprehension of complex concepts and texts. However, MLs need to practice and learn more English (or any second language).

Newer technologies such as ChatGPT are emerging and might be useful once they are tested sufficiently in multilingual classroom contexts. It is tempting to try new fads, but they might not be appropriate for all students.

Whatever technology your school selects, help teachers keep a few premises in mind:

Does this technology

- Promote MLs' active engagement?
- Help language development effectively?
- Have a scaffolded reading and writing approach?
- Provide equitable opportunities for all MLs?
- Enable coaches and teachers to learn together and exchange ideas?
- Enable coaches to work together to establish criteria for ML assessment and evaluation of the technology's impact on MLs?
- Show consistent and valuable data?

Coaches' Self-Assessments

Professional development programs help ML coaches build trust and work toward actionable, classroom-level growth. I've seen teachers who are at first pessimistic, even antagonistic, about coaching end up thanking their coaches for an incredible experience and making real changes in their teaching and student outcomes because their coach stayed engaged and used strategies proposed in this chapter and Chapters 3 and 5.

Coaching teachers takes a lot of concentration, reflection, and even personal application of SEL competencies. Self-reflection with a set of questions can guide coaches' self-assessment and self-awareness. Here are some examples adapted from Elena Aguilar (Bright Morning, 2024).

ML Coaches' Self-Assessment on Own Discourse/Communication

☐ Am I talking too much in our interactions?

☐ Are my meetings with teachers focused and purposeful?

☐ Do the teachers leave our meetings knowing exactly how to improve their teaching?

☐ Is my coaching grounded in specific data, especially related to student outcomes?

☐ Are our interactions joyful and engaging?

Coaches' Self-Assessment on Vocabulary/Discourse Next Steps

☐ Do I need to review the teachers'/coaches' manual or the training videos to fill in some little gaps?

☐ Do I need to get together with other ML coaches and do some joint reflection or ask for ideas?

☐ Do I give feedback on how to reduce teacher talk and how to give students more time to talk with peers in structured conversations?

☐ Do I provide or recommend sentence frames and table tents to generate more confident talk?

☐ Do I celebrate the small successes of teachers and students?

My greatest accomplishment thus far:

_____

_____

_____

_____

My challenge and goal:

_____

_____

_____

_____

Important Points

"A whole generation of kids still need help."

—Tom Kane, Harvard Economist

All students' reading and mathematics scores across the country in 2023 were more disappointing than those in 2022. Between 2020 and 2021 the government provided $190 billion in pandemic aid to K–12 schools, but only about 30 percent was spent on academic improvement efforts (Lobosco, 2023). By 2023, and with more funding, the schools were still struggling to catch up to where they were before the pandemic. Tutoring alone is not going to make enough difference. One major implication is that all students can benefit from learning more vocabulary and having structured opportunities to use that vocabulary in discourse during reading and before writing in all subjects.

To summarize, vocabulary must be taught all day long, in every class and every student activity, if MLs are to learn 3,500 to 5,000 words a year, and 50,000 by the end of high school. Preteaching with the seven-step strategy is a precursor to reading, academic discussions, and writing. As students read, they will learn more words. Those five words that were pretaught will cascade throughout a lesson and anchor in the students' memory as they read, discuss, and apply in follow-up learning activities.

This is how those five words at the beginning of class cascade and grow (see Figure 4.17):

1. The teacher preteaches five words.

2. The teacher presents objectives, lists social norms for peer interaction, and states where the students are to use new vocabulary.

3. Students read, and the five words are further clarified in context.

4. As students read aloud with a peer, they learn more words.

5. As students summarize verbally, they learn more words.

6. When students formulate questions from the passages they read, they learn more words and anchor vocabulary, reading comprehension, and content mastery.

7. Students participate in cooperative learning activities to apply all learning.

8. By the time they go through this sequence, students are ready to draft a writing assignment using ample vocabulary and knowledge from reading.

9. Students use the draft to practice editing and revising their work.

10. Students end a lesson/unit with self- and team assessments.

The next chapter shares how writing stems from those five words.

Figure 4.17 How Five Words Grow Throughout a Lesson

An Integrated ExC-ELL Lesson

The teacher preteaches words using
the seven steps for preteaching vocabulary.

Students read these words and more during
partner reading and summarization.

They hear these words during teacher think-alouds,

use them in conversation during class
debriefings and cooperative learning activities,

and include them in their questions and answers during
formulating questions and cooperative-competitive.

Then, students are ready to use them in their writing!

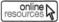 Available for download at http://resources.corwin.com/CMLExcellence

Message From a Special Guest: Making Transitions as Seamless as Possible

By Debbie Zacarian

Ask an educator about their preservice experience, and many of us recall a powerful moment . . . like when I stayed up until the wee hours of the morning to create an end-of-the-week assessment. My plans went well in the comfort of my home and poorly when they were put into action. It's helped me to understand the importance of supporting MLs in making

- Seemingly small transitions (like moving from one class activity to the next, such as from working in small groups to being assessed individually)

- Large transitions (e.g., from receiving support in English language development to being a "former English learner")

- Monumental transitions (such as fleeing a crisis, making the arduous journey to the United States, and transitioning to an American school)

When I coach administrators, teachers, and other stakeholders to support students to make transitions, we engage in a threefold cycle of inquiry:

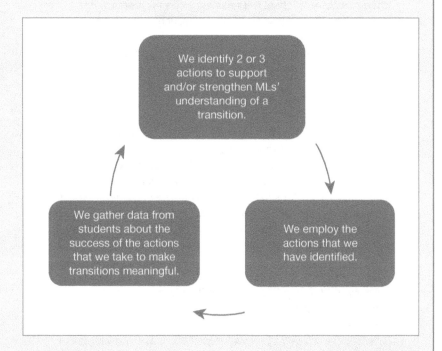

For example, I coached a group of kindergarten teachers. Each used a signal when it was time to make a transition (e.g., turning the lights on and off or clapping their hands). Kindergarten students were asked what the signal meant. Some responded that it meant stop doing an activity, put away the materials they were using, and get ready to engage in a new activity. Some responded that it meant doing one thing: stop. With these responses, we explored actions that would strengthen every students' transition from one activity to the next. Engaging in this cycle of inquiry has greatly supported educators in building smooth transitions and empowering students to do these independently.

—Debbie Zacarian, PhD, is an author and the founder of Zacarian and Associates, LLC.

(Continued)

(Continued)

From One Coach to Another

There can be no doubt that increasing students' vocabulary knowledge will have a positive impact on their success in school and beyond. In our workshops, we review the research on vocabulary knowledge, discuss word selection, and then introduce teachers to the seven steps for preteaching vocabulary. This strategy is based on research and has a proven track record of success. In the workshops, we introduce the strategy, show examples, and even model the strategy for teachers. Afterwards, teachers work in small groups to practice it themselves, "teaching" a new word to the others in their group, who play the role of students.

However, the real work of learning this instructional strategy comes after the workshop ends, when teachers must take what they've learned and use it in their own classrooms, with their own students, to teach key vocabulary from their own lessons. This is where teachers must consider not only the best practices we have introduced to them in the workshop, but also their lesson goals, the relevant content standards, the school's schedule, and the needs of individual students.

This is where coaching comes in. Many teachers will benefit from support during this phase, as they take new learning from a workshop and implement it in the classroom. I find that when I am able to observe and talk with teachers two or three weeks after they've learned the seven steps for preteaching vocabulary, this is the time when they engage the most deeply with the purpose of each step. After all, teaching is not as simple as learning a process and following it! When it comes to the seven steps, teachers grapple with how to ensure that they are not only following the process but doing so in a way that will be meaningful for their students. Here are some of the things I've asked teachers that have helped them reflect on, and improve, their vocabulary instruction:

- *Why did you select this word for explicit instruction?*
- *What did you notice after preteaching vocabulary?*
- *When did student learning occur?*
- *When you try this again in the future, is there anything you would change?*

—Leticia Trower, Professional Development Director, Margarita Calderón & Associates

Coaching Writing

From One Coach to Another: Tips for Coaches of Teachers With Multilingual Learners

I love coaching writing because it is a language domain that can be incorporated more robustly into any content area, yet it can be easily overlooked. When I help teachers discover simple ways to incorporate writing strategies into their existing classroom practices, I know that I am supporting the language development of multilingual learners as well as deepening content-area literacy for all students. Additionally, the incorporation of these practices helps to deepen real-world skills (like writing!) that are essential for students' success, both in school and beyond. Through purposeful mini-lessons, opportunities for the collaborative creation of various written products, and robust guidance as students journey through the writing process, the teacher helps to empower students to take ownership of their own learning. For me, this is perhaps the best part of getting students writing more across the curriculum—seeing students build confidence in their writing ability while actually enjoying writing!

—Rebecca Upchurch, Instructional Coach, Loudoun County Public Schools; CEO and Clarity and Mindset Coach, Higher Good Coaching

Building Literacy: Writing in the Content Areas for Multilingual Learners

Writing in the content areas means the ability to read, write, speak, and listen as a means of identification, understanding, interpretation, creation, and communication; the ability to communicate in diverse ways and with diverse audiences; and the ability to understand and use print in an increasingly text-mediated, information-rich, and digital way in a fast-changing world.

Both reading and writing demand (1) active construction of meaning, (2) interactions with core content text, (3) development of conceptual and background knowledge, and (4) development of the language, literacy, and social-emotional learning (SEL) skills and competencies described in Chapters 3 and 4.

After multilingual learners (MLs) have been taught five or so words before reading, followed by partner reading, verbal summarization, and discussions; engaged in after-reading activities to anchor vocabulary, sentence structures, and author's craft from the text; and learned key information about the topic, now they are ready to engage in interactive intensive writing.

Reading, the Science of Reading, and the focus on the differences between reading for MLs and reading for non-MLs have taken center stage recently. While it is critically important to focus on what really works in reading for MLs, the focus has eluded the other half of literacy instruction: *writing*.

The recent focus on reading has eluded the other half of literacy instruction: writing!

Reading and writing have typically been studied separately. Traditional "process writing," or the language experience approach (a popular second-language strategy), emphasizes personal experience and story generation over other genres. Now that state accountability exams are calling for more writing in science, technology, engineering, the arts, and mathematics (STEM or STEAM), teachers may find that their university preparation did not include enough about teaching writing.

Reading and Writing Are Linked

In this chapter, we want to share how easily reading and writing can be connected because writing is a perfect follow-up to reading, and writing enhances reading. "Writing can help kids become measurably better readers" (Graham et al., 2021; Shanahan, 2024b). Reading and writing share the same underlying components: vocabulary, sentence structure, paragraph structure, text features, text structures, and content knowledge. After students read a text (e.g., chapter, book, poem, article, newspaper, instructions), that text becomes a mentor text. It mentors the students into rich exciting writing that is patterned after the text they just read but given in their own voice, with their own flavor.

MLs are not writing enough!

While the research on effective writing for all students is scarce, sixty-plus studies testing various aspects/subcomponents of writing have shown positive effects. Writing has been studied in classrooms where "perhaps there were multilingual learners" (Steve Graham, personal communication, 2020) but they were never desegregated to ascertain ML participation. Nevertheless, Graham and colleagues (Graham & Hebert, 2010, 2011; Graham & Perin, 2007; Graham et al., 2021) identified the factors that contribute to writing development and writing difficulty. The researcher's concern is that there has been too much misinformation about how to teach writing: from a whole-language approach (Goodman, 1992) to writing workshops (Calkins, 2017). However, with evidence-based instruction on writing, Graham and colleagues have found more promising practices. *The evidence also supports connecting writing and reading instruction* (Graham et al., 2021).

Setting a Context for Writing

Graham and Hebert (2010) recommend setting a context and mindset for writing as well as teaching writing. For setting a context for writing, he recommends we keep these features in mind:

▶ Students should write frequently.

▶ They should be supported by teachers and peers as they write.

▶ Essential writing skills, strategies, and knowledge should be taught.

▶ Students should use word processors and other 21st century tools to write.

▶ Writing should occur in a positive and motivating environment.

Research on Writing

Under the auspices of the Carnegie Corporation of New York, Graham and Hebert (2010) published a compilation of strategies discussed in several of their studies that showed significant outcomes. The schemas and single strategies for writing were tested in multiple studies, albeit not all together in one major study. The researchers did not find a writing program that had large enough effect sizes and, in fact, found minus effects with the Lucy Calkins writing workshops (Graham & Perin, 2007; Schwartz, 2023), but they did identify these promising features with other studies:

1. Setting goals for writing

2. Teaching general as well as genre-specific strategies for planning, revising, editing, and regulating the writing process

3. Engaging students in prewriting practices for gathering, organizing, and evaluating possible writing contents and plans

4. Teaching vocabulary for writing

5. Peer assistance

6. Creating routines for students to help each other as they write

7. Teaching sentence-construction skills with sentence-combining procedures

8. Teaching paragraph-writing skills

9. Providing students with feedback about their writing and their progress learning new writing skills

10. Writing for content learning

11. Inquiry activities

Evidence That Writing Can Improve Reading and Vice Versa

Writing strategy instruction (planning/drafting, revising, and editing) has been found especially effective, as shown in Figure 5.1, for adolescents who have difficulty writing (d = 1.02) and adolescents in general (d = 0.70) (Graham & Hebert, 2010).

Figure 5.1   Writing Strategies With the Greatest Effect Sizes

1. Collaborative writing (d = .75)

2. Writing about the texts one has read (d = .63 or larger)

3. Responding to a text with personal reactions, analyzing, and interpreting text (d = .77)

4. Summarizing a text (d = .82)

5. Being taught spelling and sentence construction skills (d = .79)

The high-quality instructional strategies Graham and Hebert (2010) present also address the issue of replicability, as the replication of effects across multiple situations is the hallmark of scientific testing.

In our own components testing (Calderón, 2007), we combined Graham's evidence-based strategies with evidence-based instruction for MLs. The ExC-ELL writing model has been replicated in hundreds of classrooms across the country from New York City to Kauai, Hawaii, and Alaskan villages, as well as in Mexico, Central and South America, and Saudi Arabia.

The Instructional Model: Components of Effective Writing for Multilingual Learners

A school can structure a writing curriculum and a professional development program based on the evidence-based components we share in this chapter. We have fashioned one that teachers and students find exciting and of great benefit for all MLs and all students ($d = .75$ to $d = .82$). The explicit modeling and instruction by the teacher and the activities in teams of four help newcomers begin writing as soon as they enter a classroom, while more seasoned MLs can accelerate their writing. Non-MLs also improve their writing significantly and do better in Advanced Placement courses. A culturally responsive approach helps students to build self-confidence and self-reliance for writing and to enjoy writing extensively as they bring in their own cultures and background knowledge.

The ExC-ELL Instructional Model for Effective Writing for MLs and Peers

1. **Before Writing:**

    a. Teacher explicitly teaches self-awareness/self-regulation/self-confidence strategies.

    b. Teacher preteaches more key vocabulary, phrases, and sentence structures from the mentor text.

    c. Students do oral partner-reading and oral summarization of the mentor text.

    d. Students formulate questions about the mentor text.

    e. Teacher and students discuss text structures (descriptive, argumentative, narrative, expository).

2. **During Writing:**

    a. Teacher establishes the audience, theme, objective/standard, success criteria.

    b. Teacher reviews text to select more vocabulary, look for sentence structures to emulate, and points out potential spelling and punctuation hurdles.

(Continued)

(Continued)

3. **The Process of Writing With Peers:**

   a. Teacher models and explains the purpose of drafting.

   b. **Students draft in teams.**

   c. Teacher teaches and models editing strategies.

   d. **Students edit in teams.**

   e. Teacher teaches and models revising strategies.

   f. **Students revise in teams.**

   g. Teacher teaches and models writing conclusions.

   h. **Students write powerful conclusions in teams.**

   i. Teacher teaches and models writing a powerful title.

   j. **Students write an attention-grabbing title in teams.**

   k. Teacher teaches and models self- and peer-evaluation strategies for each segment.

   l. **Students use rubrics for self- and team evaluation.**

   m. Teacher explains voice and choice

      i. Teams select the mode of presentation.

      ii. Teams can use art or drama or any creative representation to complement their writing.

      iii. All students must take part in and contribute to team writing.

      iv. Teams self-evaluate using criteria teacher provided.

      v. Teacher and students share their writings and have a great celebration!

4. **Teacher Enhances Motivation and Increases Time on Writing:**

   a. Teacher breaks up writing process by days. Each subcomponent will take 30 to 45 minutes, and students celebrate each day!

   b. Students write with pencil and paper because it is easier to work in teams to draft their compositions. They work in teams for at least 4 consecutive weeks, 3 times per week, to internalize editing, revising, writing conventions in preparation for writing individually. Once they own the process, they can use technology for their team writing.

5. Scaffolding and Peer Self-Regulation:

   a. After four or six weeks, students can write individually if they have mastered all the aspects of the writing process. Newcomers and other MLs might still need to be paired with more capable students.

   b. When ready, students can move on to online drafting, editing, revising, and finalizing compositions.

What Coaches Do: Observe the Prewriting Process

1. Help the teacher explicitly teach self-awareness/self-regulation strategies for student self-assessment. From the SEL competencies introduced in Chapter 3, select the self-regulation and peer collaboration competencies that will work with each class. Change norms of interaction as often as necessary—from ones that are no longer needed to ones that are.

2. Observe the teacher preteach key vocabulary from the mentor text. Before students read, the teacher has taught five words, sentence starters, or transition words and placed clusters of Tier 2 words on table tents for students to see as they are writing. (ML coaches can download all these tools—example Tier 2 words, sentence starters, transition words, and so on—from www.exc-ell.com.) From the mentor text, the coach can help select and highlight the sentence structures the teacher wants to see in the students' writing.

3. Observe the students do oral partner reading and summarization and make note of the words and sentence patterns they have and those they might need.

4. Observe students formulate questions about the mentor text: In teams of four, they formulate one or two questions per team using different levels of questions (from Bloom's or other taxonomies [see Armstrong, 2010]) and test their questions with other teams using cooperative learning strategies such as the cooperative-competitive strategy (see Chapter 3).

5. Observe the teacher inform students that they now have the vocabulary, syntax examples, and information necessary to produce a composition, and ask if there is anything else they might need.

Teaching and Coaching the Process of Writing

Writing Elements Modeled by Texts and Teachers

Most writing in the core content areas will use an expository text structure (informational, descriptive, persuasive, argumentative). For MLs to write an informational text, they need to read a text with the same structure. If they read a problem–solution text, the teacher can model how to write a problem–solution composition by highlighting the features, such as the following, that would be most relevant.

Text Structure

- Awareness of audience and purpose

- Critical thinking about the process of writing (reading a mentor text, drafting, editing, revising, composing a conclusion, adding a title)

- Narrative, informational, opinion, argumentative, creative

- Patterns of organization (description, sequence, cause and effect, compare and contrast, problem and solution)

Writing Craft

- Word choice (Tier 2 word specificity: *walked on, trampled, stomped*)

- Literary devices (onomatopoeia, foreshadowing, metaphor, simile, allusion, paradox, symbolism, hyperbole, connotation, epigraph, allegory, alliteration, analogy, imagery, parallelism)

- Text features (bold letters, highlighting, pictures, illustrations, charts)

- Paragraph structure (topic sentence, support, conclusion; beginning, middle, end; make a central argument, provide evidence, explain point and evidence, link to the next paragraph)

- Linking and transition words (*initially, additionally, in addition, moreover, nevertheless, albeit, notwithstanding, however, if . . . then, therefore, due to*)

Syntax: Grammar and Syntactic Awareness

- Complete sentences

- Sentence combining and sentence elaboration (subordinate, prepositional, and adverbial clauses; incorporate examples, evidence, or anecdotes to develop main points)

- Punctuation (period, comma, parentheses, brackets, quotation mark, exclamation mark, hyphen, dash, apostrophe, colon, semicolon)

- Spelling (double consonants; *ie* versus *ei*; plurals; adding suffixes—keep the final *e*; *-ence, -ance*)

Vignette: ML Coach Can Observe and Give Impromptu Information During the Process

During the writing process, Mr. McGraw and his ML coach Mr. Moran observe by walking around the room to look for areas of needs as students draft and revise. When their observations identify instances of incomplete sentences, the teacher asks the students to pause their writing for a mini-lesson. The mini-lesson is on comparing an incomplete sentence (Went into the river to hide) *to a complete one* (The frightened soldier went into a shallow part of the river to hide from the soldiers). *Afterwards, the students resumed their writing, integrating more description and making sure they had a subject-verb-object agreement.*

Sample Writing Strategies

A strategy called *Write Around* is highly preferred by content teachers because it facilitates all stages of the writing process and is exciting for students because they get to work with peers (Calderón et al., 2011). Once the teams have drafted a full page, they can continue with the sequence of editing, revising, and adding an introduction, conclusion, and title.

When introducing this strategy, remind newcomers that they can use their primary language or translanguaging (see Chapter 4) in the drafting stage if that allows them to participate fully in the writing. During the editing stage, they will be able to change what they want or what the teacher and peers suggest into English.

Phase 1: Drafting

- State the goal and time for drafting.
- State the text type and author's purpose for meeting this goal: informative, persuasive, narrative, personal, research, argumentative, problem and solution, cause and effect, compare and contrast, describe and define, sequence and reference.
- Students pull their desks together in quads or triads or even in straight lines if classrooms are set up that way.

Steps for Drafting in Teams

1. Students clear their desks. The teacher provides a prompt for all students.

2. Each student in the team needs one sheet of paper and one pencil.

3. Each team member copies the teacher-provided prompt on their sheet of paper, completes the sentence, and then passes the paper to the right.

4. Each student reads the sentence on the paper they just received, writes one additional related sentence based on the previous sentence, and passes the paper to the right.

5. Students read all previous sentences and add another related sentence each time they receive the sheet, then pass it to the right. As students add to the work, they try to use Tier 2 and 3 words from the mentor text. They know they can add more when editing/revising. The important thing to remember is that at this stage we want them to get ideas on paper and not worry about spelling or other things they can edit and revise later.

6. Students continue passing papers around and writing until they fill at least three-quarters of a page or a full page. However, writing may continue beyond this point, concluding only when the teacher says to stop (Calderón, 2007; see also Figure 5.2).

Figure 5.2   Observation Protocol for Drafting

✓ CHECK OR USE 1–4	WRITE AROUND PHASE 1 FOR DRAFTING	NOTES
	Students clear their desks promptly.	
	The teacher provides a prompt for all to start the writing.	
	Each team member copies the teacher-provided prompt on their sheet of paper, completes the sentence, then passes the paper to the right.	
	Each student reads the sentence on the paper they just received, writes one additional related sentence based on the previous sentence, and passes the paper to the right.	
	Students read all previous sentences and add another related sentence each time they receive the sheet, then pass it to the right.	
	Students continue passing papers around and writing until they fill at least three-quarters of a page or a full page.	

Vignette: Students Engaged in Write Around

Mrs. Williams, with the help of her coach, distributed students in heterogenous teams of four. She came up with five teams, each with one ML. All seemed perfect. Her coach had come in a day before to go over the list of materials she would need (paper, pencils, table tents, timer). She had rehearsed the process in her mind several times. Just as she was about to begin, the English as a second language (ESL) teacher brought two newcomers who had no English and of course had not read the mentor text or learned the key vocabulary. She took a deep breath and placed each in a different team. She spoke to the teams who would be their peers and asked them to be "nice" and help as much as possible. Her coach suggested she have a language peer ask the newcomers if they knew something about climate change. They did know. They had lived through hurricanes and changes in climate in their countries. Mrs. Williams's coach, who spoke a little Spanish, told the students to write in Spanish when it was their turn. That made the students stop feeling apprehensive and feel that they belonged. It also made their peers more comfortable not having to skip them or show them what to write.

Teacher and Coach Reflect

Mrs. Williams told her coach that she was extremely grateful for her help with this unexpected situation. Her nerves were on edge enough having to try something new, and with this surprise she was sure she would've lost it if her coach hadn't been there to help solve the problem. The coach was glad to have been there. They planned Phase 2 and decided that Mrs. Williams would focus on the team editing while the coach would facilitate the newcomers' participation.

Phase 2: Editing

When the teacher calls time, students take turns reading aloud to their group the draft they have in their hands. There are no specific individual owners of the writing, as each team member has contributed to each paper. After reading, either students work with all four papers in their group to edit, or they choose one paper that all four members work on editing. Joint editing helps students to find more editing needs, be more precise, and learn more from each other.

One Easy Editing Strategy: Ratiocination

Ratiocination means to form judgments by a process of logic (see Figure 5.3). Students can form judgments about their editing by asking questions: "Should we substitute this easy word for a more sophisticated one?" "Is this a complete sentence? What does it need?" "Do we have capital letters where they belong?" "What about spelling? Should we circle words we're not sure of?" Some students will write a sentence a mile long. Others will forget a verb or a noun. During this phase, students need to be taught sentence and paragraph structure and to write for different purposes and genre.

Students start by checking for just one thing—for example, boxing the first word of every sentence followed by deciding which one they want to "upgrade." The next time they write, they add another strategy. We don't want them to feel overwhelmed by attempting to edit too many things.

Some teachers prefer to edit twice: after the first draft and after revising with another strategy called Cut 'n' Grow, outlined later in this chapter (Calderón, 1984, 1986, 1990, 1994, 1996).

Distribute a ratiocination chart such as Figure 5.4. In the last cell, students or the teacher can add specific needs for this assignment. Maybe each team is working on something different. The teacher can differentiate by assigning a specific strategy to a student who needs extra practice with punctuation or other features.

Figure 5.3 Ratiocination Examples

ON A COMPUTER	PAPER AND PENCIL	MEANING
Italicize	Box	First word (or phrase) in every sentence Decide: Keep or change to sophisticated transition word or connector
Bold	Circle	"To be" verbs: *is, am, are, was, were, be, being, been* Decide: Keep or change to active verb
Underline	Underline	Simple (Tier 1) words Decide: Keep or substitute with more sophisticated (Tier 2) word
Highlight alternating sentences	Highlight alternating sentences	Highlight alternating sentences to show structure and length variety
Individualized	Individualized	Student-centered differentiation

Source: Calderón (2007, 2022). Graphic by Nanci Esparza.

An Activity for You

Look for something you or one of your students have written lately. Use a couple of ratiocination strategies.

What Coaches Do for Observation and Feedback

There are several things the coach and teacher can agree on for the observation-feedback focus. First, there is the sequence of the editing. For the first time students try ratiocination, it is easier to start with boxing every first word/phrase of every sentence. This will show repetitions (e.g., *The, They, I, Because, And*), which could be changed to more sophisticated words. For the second time they draft and use ratiocination, students can circle end punctuation to see if it is the right way to end a sentence or if the punctuation is missing. Thereafter, the teacher can ask them to underline verbs, circle capital letters, highlight incomplete sentences, or do anything the teacher sees that students need to work on.

Teacher feedback to students is key at this stage. Teachers need to help students see feedback as information rather than just a score or a grade. Feedback is not a score or a grade. We need to help students develop this idea that feedback from the teacher and from peers is part of reviewing and improving one's writing. Once they are comfortable working with peers, ask them to give each other feedback using a rubric or your suggestions.

Figure 5.4 Observation Protocol for Ratiocination

✓ CHECK OR USE 1–4	TEACHING EDITING WITH RATIOCINATION	NOTES
	Teacher models and teaches each ratiocination strategy.	
	Student teams approach and accomplish the task fluidly.	
	SEL competencies are stated by the teacher and used by students (self-management, decision making, social awareness, relationship building).	
	The teacher conducts a mini-lesson on punctuation, capitalization, sentence structures, or other necessary topics.	
	The teacher provides feedback, and students understand the importance of feedback and act on it.	

online resources 🔖 Available for download at http://resources.corwin.com/CMLExcellence

Phase 3: Revising With Cut 'n' Grow

Revising complete sentences and paragraphs by adding evidence or quotations and restating claims or counterclaims requires that students ponder, reread, research, and make decisions as to what to add to a composition. (See Figure 5.5.)

1. Students find a sentence that needs elaboration: evidence, claim, or counterclaim.

2. Students cut their compositions right after the sentence where they are going to add evidence from the text.

3. The additional sentence(s) are written on a colored sheet of paper. Once written, the students tape the rest of their composition onto the colored sheet.

4. Students reread their improved compositions.

Phase 4: Writing a Conclusion and Title for the Composition

1. Add a powerful ending or conclusion.

2. Give it a title—an attention grabber!

3. Select a reader to share it with the class.

4. Prepare your volunteer to read it to the class. Help the volunteer practice reading with prosody and enthusiasm.

Figure 5.5   Protocol for Revising With Cut 'n' Grow

✓ CHECK OR USE 1–4	TEACHING REVISING WITH CUT 'N' GROW	NOTES
	The teacher models and teaches Cut 'n' Grow to improve upon student-selected sentences.	
	Student teams approach and accomplish each task in a timely manner.	
	The teacher conducts a mini-lesson on sentence elaboration, adding evidence, making claims or counterclaims, specific criteria, or other necessary topics for narrative and creative writing.	
	SEL competencies are stated by the teacher and used by students throughout the process (self-management, decision making, social awareness, relationship building).	
	The teacher models and students write powerful conclusions and titles.	
	Products are read and posted.	

An Activity for You

What other SEL skills/competencies are MLs using during each of the writing stages?

The Instructional Model: Creative Writing

All students enjoy writing about themselves, their families, or their friends. Identity stories benefit the writers and the readers of their stories because they get to know each other better. Have students read autobiographies or family histories. Brainstorm a list of words that students might want to use.

The Rip 'n' Rite Strategy

Rip 'n' Rite is a highly interactive strategy (see Figure 5.6). This is a strategy for creative writing, narrative, or fiction writing that follows the sequence of drafting, editing, and revising but adds more discourse and creativity. For example, the Rip 'n' Rite strategy is conducted in teams of three or four. *The purpose of this team strategy is to generate a lot of verbal discourse* before students start writing. After they have ripped pieces of paper in creative ways, each student takes a turn describing that piece—what it looks like and what it might represent if they were to write a story. Encourage as much talk as possible.

Figure 5.6   Rip 'n' Rite for Discourse and Creative Writing

The Rip 'n' Rite Process

1. Each person rips sheets of paper into creative pieces. The more colors, the better!

2. Each person shares one piece with their team and talks about it: What does it look like?

3. The group designs a story, usually about the topic they have been reading.

4. The story must include the story elements and/or vocabulary the teacher specifies.

5. Students have criteria to meet such as using Tier 2 and 3 words, using elements of plot, having rich descriptions of characters, and creating a powerful conclusion and title.

6. All groups share their stories.

Seventh graders learn to be creative.

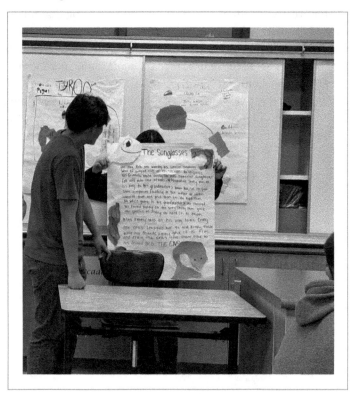

An Activity for You

Follow the steps for the Rip 'n' Rite strategy with a family member and come up with a colorful masterpiece.

Have fun with it!

The RAFT Strategy

Culturally and linguistically responsive instruction means students and their families can tap into their love of writing and sharing about their culture. Rip 'n' Rite and the RAFT strategy, described in the next section, are ideal for MLs to be creative as they integrate their background knowledge and their interests with new school knowledge.

The RAFT Process

RAFT is an acronym for *role, audience, format,* and *topic.* This strategy can be done individually or in pairs. It also enables creativity as students consolidate the vocabulary they learned, the information and ideas they gained from reading, and techniques from drafting, editing, and revising.

The process builds on imagination and student choice as they make decisions for each of the four parts (see Figure 5.7).

R = Role (Who are you as a writer?): Allows students to take on a variety of roles to explore different points of view

A = Audience (To whom are you writing?): The audience must be clearly defined.

F = Format (What form will the writing take?): Essay, speech, letter, dialogue, memo, or another format.

T = Topic (What is the subject?): Must be narrow enough so students are not overwhelmed.

Figure 5.7 Examples of How Students Organize RAFTs

R = ROLE	A = AUDIENCE	F = FORMAT	T = TOPIC
News reporter	Politicians	News article	Global warming
Astronomer	Seniors	Travel guide	Journey through the solar system
Acute triangle	Obtuse triangle	Letter	Differences among triangles
Famous medical doctor	Nobel prize	Acceptance speech	Staying healthy

What Coaches Do for Rip 'n' Rite, RAFT, and Cooperative Writing

Coaches can support teachers by helping to

- ☐ Create partnerships and groups.
- ☐ Make sure that groups are of mixed language proficiency and academic knowledge.
- ☐ Choose mini-lessons to teach based on student work.
- ☐ Find mentor texts as exemplars.
- ☐ Create table tents to support student learning.
- ☐ Observe groups to see that all students are writing.

Coaches can observe and give feedback on

- ☐ Students writing cooperatively in small groups
- ☐ Authentic and meaningful writing
- ☐ Social-emotional skills taught through mini-lessons
- ☐ Teacher modeling of writing processes

The Instructional Model: Writing in Pairs or Teams for Multilingual Learners

Cooperative learning is particularly beneficial for any student learning a second language. Cooperative learning activities promote peer interaction, which facilitates the development of language and the learning of concepts and content (Hattie & Clarke, 2019). It is important to assign MLs to different teams so that they can benefit from English-language role models. MLs learn to express themselves with greater confidence when working in small teams. In addition to learning more vocabulary, MLs benefit from observing how their peers learn and solve problems. Cooperative learning also enables the practice and development of SEL competencies.

Higher-Order Tasks/Topics for Cooperative Learning in Teams

- ▶ Asking questions and defining problems
- ▶ Developing and using models for STEM

- Planning and carrying out science investigations

- Analyzing, interpreting data, and writing a report

- Summarizing using mathematics and computational thinking

- Constructing explanations and designing solutions

- Engaging in argument from evidence

- Obtaining, evaluating, and communicating information

To Summarize: Implications for Educators

Graham and Perin (2007) did a meta-analysis of writing in Grades 6 to 12. The findings from this meta-analysis yielded these important implications:

1. If teachers and policymakers want to improve the writing of secondary students, then they need to do more than just increase how much time students spend writing.

2. It is critical that teachers explicitly teach planning, drafting, revising, and editing, as well as how to construct more complex sentences and apply grammar correctly. For some students, instruction to improve their spelling, handwriting, or keyboarding can also be advantageous.

3. The aims of writing must be made clear through goal setting for the teacher and students, as well as providing both with feedback and having them assist each other as they compose.

4. Set in place procedures that help secondary students learn more about what constitutes good writing. This includes providing them with good models of writing to emulate, asking them to observe others as they write or react to others' writing, and teaching them about the purposes and construction of different types of text.

5. Secondary students write better using tools that allow them to compose multimodal text. It also includes the use of computer-assisted instruction as a means for teaching writing. For MLs, we highly recommend that they start with paper and pencil before relying on artificial intelligence (AI) programs such as ChatGPT or similar tools or use both approaches for different purposes.

6. If teachers and policymakers want to enhance secondary students' reading, then writing instruction needs to become a consistent and valued part of middle and high school students' education.

Points to Remember

Instructional coaches are most helpful to teachers at this stage of the coaching cycle if they can explain to teachers the effect size of strategies in the writing playbook. For example, Knight (2019) reminds us that if a teacher sets a goal for students' writing, the coach can explain that teacher clarity has an effect size of d = 0.75, formative evaluation has an effect size of d = 0.90, feedback has an effect size of d = 0.75, and in combination clarity, formative evaluation, and feedback represent a powerful set of strategies that may be used to hit an achievement goal.

There might still be many teachers who have had little training in writing in their college education courses or in-district professional development. They will need extra support and understanding. Perhaps the most difficult realization will be that MLs and all students need to be taught explicitly the skills and strategies of writing. Science, social studies, language arts, and STEM/STEAM teachers will need to see the connections among reading, writing, and knowledge development. Writing to learn mathematics, science, and social studies entails a mix of higher-order analyses, argumentative writing, summarizing, and explaining. Writing about the content in each class improves student learning.

Points to Remember About MLs' Writing

- ▶ Students need to do more than just increase time on writing.

- ▶ Writing is not just for English language arts or ESL/English language development (ELD); it's for all subject areas.

- ▶ No commercial writing program has been proven to be effective with MLs.

- ▶ Instead of buying or relying on a writing program, develop teacher capacity through evidence-based writing strategies.

An evidence-based model for developing MLs' writing continues to be effective across all grades and subjects. Coupled with insights from researchers, the ExC-ELL model can be an effective tool for all students because of its breadth of application.

The ExC-ELL Writing Process

A variety of techniques have been coalesced into a model that has been tested with teachers, coaches, and MLs. This model is a place to begin building on writing techniques. It is flexible enough to try pieces at a time and gradually build a supermodel.

The features of the ExC-ELL writing approach shown in Figure 5.8 can be used to build a teacher's writing approach and an observation protocol. The reading–writing connection improves both.

Figure 5.8   Features of the ExC-ELL Writing Approach

THE ExC-ELL WRITING PROCESS	THE ExC-ELL WRITING ESSENTIALS
1. Comprehensive framework	1. Explicit teaching
2. Based on second language and writing theory and research	2. Teacher modeling
	3. Peer collaboration
3. Evidence based	4. Embedded skill instruction
4. Proven track record	5. Self- and peer evaluation
5. Integrates with all subjects and grade levels	6. Gradual release
	7. Goal oriented

 Available for download at http://resources.corwin.com/CMLExcellence

Message From a Special Guest: A Multidimensional Approach to Coaching for Effective Multilingual Instruction

By Rubí Patricia Flores

Teaching MLs is a complex task. It requires a unique multidimensional approach to coaching that goes beyond the instructional practices and resources necessary to deliver ML instruction. Professional learning for educators of multilingual students requires more than financial, physical, and cognitive resources. This process also requires a strategic investment in the development of a social justice and advocacy mindset, assets-based empathy and sociocultural competence, and the emotional intelligence of educators.

Developing a Social Justice and Advocacy Mindset

It is no secret that our educational system has been and continues to be greatly influenced by monolingual policies, initiatives, political movements, and English-centric instructional philosophies. We've seen it time and time again across the history of our nation: policies that limit access to multilingual education, practices that encourage a one-size-fits-all approach to literacy instruction, and anti-immigrant political movements. These all reflected in the philosophies and approaches schools adopt to implement language and literacy instruction for MLs. To dispel these biased and prejudiced narratives, coaching for the development of a social

(Continued)

(Continued)

justice and advocacy mindset is essential. Educators serving MLs must learn to critically examine new and existing educational policies in order to identify the ones that aim to undervalue and strip the linguistic assets and identities of MLs. Through this coaching, they can be encouraged to engage in the much-needed redesign of a truly just and equitable educational system.

Assets-Based Empathy and Sociocultural Competence

Every ML has a unique language-learning story that must be unpacked by the educators serving them to establish positive relationships with students. As most students are served by monolingual educators who may not share the same multilingual experiences, there must be an intentional focus to coach educators of MLs to develop an assets-based sense of empathy and sociocultural competence. For example, create a student-centered approach of teaching and learning focused on conducting surveys, interviews, or home visits to learn about the cultural and linguistic assets that students bring to the classroom. Data can be analyzed to identify similarities and differences between students' lived experiences and those of the educator.

With guidance, educators can identify the points of connection to the potential, the resilience, the aspirations, and the human need to be seen, heard, and valued that they share with MLs. When educators are aware of the complexity of learning a new language, learning content in a foreign language, and learning how to navigate the social norms of a new culture, they will be more likely to create welcoming and responsive learning environments that will empower students to embrace their multilingual/ multicultural identities and to develop a sense of belonging.

Emotional Intelligence

Coaching educators of MLs requires the need to cultivate the emotional intelligence of educators. Developing learning experiences that will embed the academic, linguistic, and sociocultural needs of MLs is an intricate process. There's often a socioemotional and cognitive toll to becoming a highly effective educator of MLs. It is not uncommon for educators to feel discouraged by the amount of time and effort that planning for effective ML instruction requires. Professional learning and coaching must also aim to address and prevent the possibility of teacher burnout.

We're experiencing a heightened emphasis on learning recovery after the COVID-19 pandemic. Although we cannot oversimplify the planning process required, we can ensure that we are arming teachers with effective strategies to manage stress, to develop self-confidence, and to manage their emotions. Some strategies may include providing clear and effective instructional models and expectations to facilitate the planning process for

ML instruction, coaching teachers through collaborative planning cycles to alleviate workload, providing space for teachers of MLs to share their successes publicly and to serve as models for others, and conducting check-in conversations about issues affecting MLs. Multilingual instruction is truly effective when educators feel emotionally prepared to handle the workload and the political aspect of language education. Coaching in these settings requires that we think beyond the language and the content, and that we adopt a multidimensional approach that also takes into consideration the sociopolitical, sociocultural, and socioemotional aspects of teaching and learning.

Rubí Patricia Flores is the director of professional learning at the California Association for Bilingual Education (CABE) and has coached in dual-language and ELD classrooms across California and in Texas.

From One Coach to Another

As I reflect on times spent in classrooms observing teachers implement components of the ExC-ELL writing model, there are some common elements that come to mind for those who really excel (pun intended!). Teachers who actively implement the focused strategy have procedures in place, and it is obvious that students are not receiving the instructions for the first time. (Note: Teachers see the value in the training and are on board with implementation!) Additionally, teachers have their materials ready for the lesson, and students are quickly paired for the strategy and motivated to start. (Note: Teachers know their students' interests and needs and how to partner them accordingly.) Students are able to drive their learning, communicating effectively with each other to progress on the assignment while the teacher monitors, assesses, and clarifies among student groups as needed. (Note: Teachers have created a learning community!) This is further demonstrated when students are able to give and receive constructive feedback. Well done!

In order to grow and attain higher levels of achievement, we must promote an environment that feels safe and supported. This is our time as a coach to encourage and empower. Additionally, it is a time to clarify points from the training. Whether a seasoned professional or a beginning teacher, those who implement the ExC-ELL model, albeit in bite-sized chunks at first, will experience results among every part of their classroom population as never before!

—Karen Solis, Instructional Coach, North Carolina

Creating a Whole-School Approach to Coaching

CHAPTER #6

From One Administrator to Another

Instructional coaching in education has a clear purpose: improve outcomes for learners. Coaching is a powerful activity that is used to support teachers to learn and develop skills that will increase their ability to perform at higher levels, successfully implement learned strategies, and have greater outcomes in targeted subject areas. Just as the quality of teaching determines student success, the quality and structure of the coaching determines how well coaching succeeds with teachers. Coaching depends on several factors: the clarity of purpose of coaching; the coach's knowledge and skills and the conditions in which coaching occurs; and the active support of the administrators in order to ensure effective implementation and sustainability of instructional programs and practices.

The ExC-ELL coaching framework described in this book incorporates these essential components in an effective coaching cycle that anchors the work in the professional development teachers have received on vocabulary, reading, and writing in all subject areas. It is also designed to be relational, builds positive and trusting relationships, and has a direct impact on classroom culture, climate, and student achievement. Whether in person or virtually, the ExC-ELL coaching framework gives teachers clarity on the purpose and goals of coaching and reassures them that it is not judgmental nor evaluative but supportive, interactive, reflective, and collaborative. To have a productive coaching relationship, teachers and coaches need to trust one another and respect each other professionally. Teachers must believe that the coach supports them, and that the coach's top priority is increased achievement for all students.

In my career as a former teacher and administrator, coaching was always random and arbitrary, lacked structure, and was only for ineffective teachers who needed to be fixed. I have thoroughly enjoyed coaching using the ExC-ELL model primarily due to having direct access to the classroom and focusing on specific teaching practices that all teachers should implement. As a result, I have observed some outstanding instructional practices that have been engaging and inclusive of multilingual learners (MLs) and produced higher-level writing skills, even from newcomers. What I like most about the ExC-ELL model is that it requires that trainers and coaches work collaboratively (with school leaders) to plan, implement, and assess school change initiatives to ensure alignment with and focus on intended results, and to monitor the transfer learnings from professional development into action.

The principal–trainer–coach relationship is the heart of the program. Without good relationships with administrators, teachers, and coaches, the work cannot get done, nor can the ExC-ELL strategies that MLs and all students need be implemented with fidelity and sustained over time. I only wish that I had this framework when I was an administrator. I would have had a greater impact on overall school climate and student achievement.

—Hector Montenegro, EdD, Former Teacher, Principal, and Superintendent, Austin, Texas

Coaching for Quality Instruction and Impact on Multilingual Learners

When the whole school is involved, all students and educators excel. No matter how effective the professional development is in theory, it needs to be linked to student learning in an educational setting to effect real school change (Guskey, 1997).

A whole-school implementation needs at least two or three years to show great results. Educators can begin implementation with one component. For example, the language component (vocabulary) can be mapped out for observing and discussing transfer. During the first year, some teachers can implement one strategy well while others reach an exemplary stage with multiple strategies. Exemplary teachers are quite willing to have other teachers come and observe their teaching, and they themselves become excellent peer coaches. A simple graphic organizer focusing on transfer, such as Figure 6.1, which uses vocabulary as an example, can be filled out by the teachers themselves or with the help of their ML coaches.

Figure 6.1   Example of Vocabulary Indicators for Tracking Transfer and Impact on Multilingual Learners

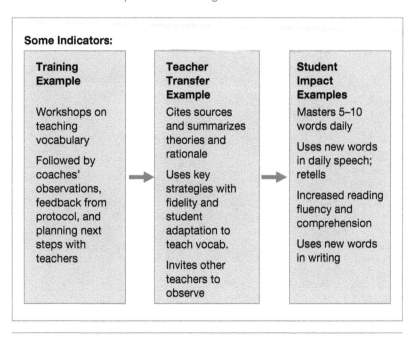

Some Indicators:

Training Example	Teacher Transfer Example	Student Impact Examples
Workshops on teaching vocabulary

Followed by coaches' observations, feedback from protocol, and planning next steps with teachers | Cites sources and summarizes theories and rationale

Uses key strategies with fidelity and student adaptation to teach vocab.

Invites other teachers to observe | Masters 5–10 words daily

Uses new words in daily speech; retells

Increased reading fluency and comprehension

Uses new words in writing |

online resources   Available for download at http://resources.corwin.com/CMLExcellence

After each workshop, collaborative inquiry takes place, such as by using Figure 6.2, to analyze data from observations, coaching reports, student products, surveys, and other evidence of implementation to fill columns 1 and 2. For column 3 on student impact and further needs, record the grades MLs are getting in each subject, the results of interim district or state exams, and students' perspectives and suggestions from random interviews.

Figure 6.2   Collaborative Inquiry Organizer to Measure Quality Implementation and Transfer

DISCUSSION	STATUS	STUDENT IMPACT AND FURTHER NEEDS
1. Was the workshop effective?		
2. How many teachers are implementing?		
3. Are students learning and applying strategies?		
4. Is the coaching being implemented systematically?		

(Continued)

(Continued)

DISCUSSION	STATUS	STUDENT IMPACT AND FURTHER NEEDS
5. Which instructional strategies/data sources are being used/not used?		
6. Are the teachers meeting their own goals?		
7. Teacher exemplary practices		
8. Student exemplary practices		
9. Student challenges		
10. Coach challenges		
11. Coach successes		
12. Leadership observations		

 Available for download at http://resources.corwin.com/CMLExcellence

What Coaches Do to Track Coaching Impact

Various types of data can be collected to measure teacher, coach, and student impact and transfer. There are multiple ways to create valid data.

1. **Features of the coaching program.** Use these guiding questions to collect information about the program to measure what is in place.

   ▶ Did we meet the goals and objectives of the coaching program?

   ▶ What are the program components that worked?

   ▶ What pre- and post-implementation student data do we have to show impact?

   ▶ Is our observation protocol valid and reliable? Data for evidence?

2. **Observation protocols.** Collect observation protocols/logs or reports of observations.

   ▶ Did we analyze and summarize patterns?

   ▶ Where do we see the most impact?

3. **Teacher and administrator surveys.** Construct surveys to gather information about perceptions of success and areas for growth.

4. **Personal narratives by teachers.** Teachers might want to write their own narratives about their experiences and the benefits they derived along with recommendations for coaches and themselves.

5. **Personal narratives by coaches.** Coaches might want to write their own narratives about their experiences and the benefits they derived along with recommendations for the school and themselves.

6. **Student narratives.** Ask teams of three or four MLs to meet with you to help come up with ideas on how to improve linguistic and academic success for all.

7. **Artifacts.** Collect multimodal evidence of learning: portfolios, visuals, infographics, and PowerPoints, as well as technological, musical, and artistic representations.

8. **Case studies.** Gather descriptions of success stories of teachers who have experienced significant growth and student outcomes.

A comprehensive report aggregating quantitative and qualitative data should be drafted, then routed to leadership and participating teachers. A final report can be used to show the success of the program—coaching outcomes, teacher outcomes, and student outcomes—with a plan on how to improve where necessary.

What type of coach(es) does your school need? See Figure 6.3.

Figure 6.3 Types of Coaches

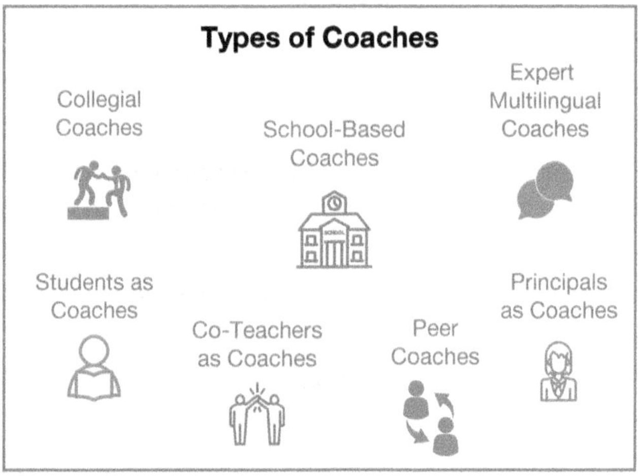

Source: Graphic by Leticia M. Trower

Peter DeWitt (2023) emphasizes that coaching has the potential to benefit the coach and the one being coached. When it comes to effective instruction for MLs, the coach learns as much as the teachers. The co-construction of learning and improving practice is the ultimate goal for all educators.

"If you're coaching and not learning, you're not coaching" (DeWitt, 2023).

The Power of Relationships

Relationships are a cornerstone of social-emotional learning (SEL) that help even the most reticent newcomer feel welcomed and the most reluctant teacher find the strength to try new ways of teaching MLs. Multilingual/multicultural coaching can be exciting but at times not so easy. Ideally, ML coaches will be working in schools where a social-emotional program is in place, and it is working well. A functioning social-emotional program will help students and adults nurture valuable skills and build supportive environments. SEL creates a solid foundation for MLs, as well as their teachers and their teachers' coaches, to flourish.

What Coaches Do to Reflect and Build Relationships

▶ Know the strengths, interests, goals, academic needs, and SEL needs of students, teachers, fellow coaches, administrators, and families.

▶ Identify what would make a good relationship with the teachers you coach.

▶ Discover what your usual coaching communication approach is and whether it is time to change it.

▶ Pinpoint three goals you would like to accomplish this year and how you plan to get there. Identify how you will know when you have met the goals.

▶ Investigate some SEL competencies everyone in the school can use.

▶ Check in with yourself and your colleagues. What is working? What are the challenges? How can you support one another?

These collaborative reflections will lay the foundation for strong relationships at the school that will serve the well-being of everyone. Collaborative inquiry becomes the mainstay for supporting students' social and mental wellness, assurance of belonging, and academic learning.

Collaborative inquiry is a cyclical process that begins with a problem of practice or an inquiry question focusing on an issue educators want to solve. What I have found is that leaders often want teachers to engage in the process, but leaders don't engage in the process often enough (Knight, 2023).

Collaborative Inquiry in Multilingual Settings

As both DeWitt (2023) and Knight (2023) have stated many times, reciprocal learning builds relationships between the coach and the person being coached. This leads to collaborative inquiry where teachers will feel more comfortable about being coached. Coaches will feel more confident about approaching teachers with the formidable topics of language instruction, equity, self-discovery of biases toward certain students, and the value of working together to make a stronger, more successful school.

Since not all secondary school teachers are prepared to implement responsive teaching and learning approaches, this book has featured a planned comprehensive process to help teachers and coaches develop a system, mindset, and practices that are ML-centered and key to improving the education of their peers as well as their own.

Teachers, coaches, administrators, and parents must work together to explore the status and views of MLs. Through collective inquiry, they determine where the whole school needs to go in their quest for academic and SEL plans. The chapters in this book have offered various tools for gathering important student data and relevant school data. As the schools proceed with implementation, it will soon become obvious that *the best formative data come from coaching observations*. Defining success criteria for each component (vocabulary, discourse, reading, writing, SEL, and cooperative learning) is key for observations and data collection. Cycles of inquiry-focused data on MLs can be very valuable for updating school and individual student plans, as well as the coaching component.

A whole-school approach brings all teachers, coaches, and school leaders together to focus on ML outcomes (see Figure 6.4). Everyone participates in learning cycles on the same components that work for MLs and all other students.

Figure 6.4   A Whole-School Approach to Multilingual Learner Instruction in Every Classroom

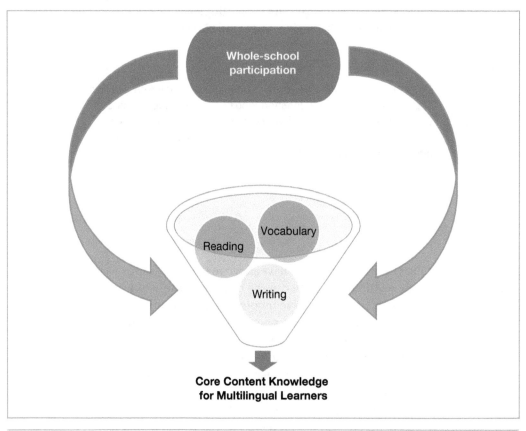

 Available for download at http://resources.corwin.com/CMLExcellence

Improving outcomes for the range of multilingual students from newcomers to long-term English learners (LTELs) requires teachers to develop the mindset, cultural understanding, and pedagogical expertise to advance their MLs' success and well-being. This does not happen in a single year of teacher preparation or with one or two additional professional learning sessions. It is a multiyear endeavor. Building relevant skills and implementing them is part of an ongoing professional trajectory that requires the investment of time and funding to support teachers through this journey. The role of the school's leadership is to provide funding, time for planning, and collaboration among teachers and ML coaches, as well as support that builds a whole-school system of caring and enacting their best for MLs.

The Power of Teacher Learning Communities

Where do these collective inquiries take place? They can take place in collegial teams or professional learning communities (PLCs). We call them teacher learning communities (TLCs) (Calderón & Carreón, 2001). Little

(1990) noted that collaboration is a powerful way to change teaching practice when it involves joint work that includes critical inquiry, sustained scrutiny of practice, analysis, and debate in search of improvement. Darling-Hammond and Richardson (2009) found that professional development is most effective when it is intensive and sustained over an extended period, involves participants in collaborative learning, and empowers teachers to take part in school decision making. Learning new knowledge, applying it to practice, and reflecting on results with colleagues are beneficial professional development practices. Hattie (2009) asserted that a powerful way to learn is "when teachers meet to discuss, evaluate, and plan their teaching in light of the feedback evidence" (p. 239).

The premises proposed by Judith Little (1990) were the basis of a study in a dual-language school where bilingual and nonbilingual teachers worked together to deliver 50 percent of instruction in English and 50 percent in Spanish. As part of the professional development cycle, all teachers participated in TLCs as a complementary support system for teachers by teachers (Calderón, 1999; Calderón & Carreón, 2001). Since that study, the TLCs continue to focus only on MLs' instructional practices and typically meet for thirty minutes to discuss implementation and problems, share what works, and celebrate successes (Calderón & Minaya-Rowe, 2003; Calderón et al., 2022).

Teacher Learning Communities

TLCs are places and spaces where teachers jointly study their craft and sustain a quality implementation.

- ✓ Teachers analyze observation data from the coaching protocol focusing on teacher and student learning progressions and outcomes.
- ✓ Teachers examine MLs' performance data across the various content areas: literature, social studies, mathematics, science, and so on.
- ✓ Teachers identify student strengths and needs.
- ✓ Teachers discuss equity and potential biases.
- ✓ Teachers celebrate successes together.

Sample TLC Agenda

- ▶ 5 minutes for sharing successes
- ▶ 5 minutes for problem solving
- ▶ 10–15 minutes for instructional demos or for analyzing student work
- ▶ 5 minutes for celebration

Source: Calderón (1999).

Impact of TLCs on Reading Gains

In successful TLCs, teachers discuss closing the disparity gaps by being more results-oriented and setting and achieving high expectations for every student. They discuss issues of implementation and transfer, equity, and high expectations among the topics of instruction.

We (Calderón, 2016) studied three TLCs in different schools that were interested in improving reading and wanted reading to be the focus of all TLCs that year. In school 1, the TLCs met once a week; in school 2, they met every other week; in school 3, they met once a month. The three school cohorts met for thirty minutes each time.

At the end of the year, we measured student growth in reading, and as one can imagine, the frequency of meetings made a difference in student gains as shown in Figure 6.5. This graphic is typically shared in administrators' and coaches' work sessions because it sets the stage for wanting to learn more about transfer and the value of giving time to teachers and coaches to make meaning of their challenges and successes (Calderón, 2016; Calderón et al., 2022). The more quality time teachers spend in TLCs, the higher students' improvement in reading.

Figure 6.5   Correlation Between Time in Teacher Learning
Communities and Reading Gains

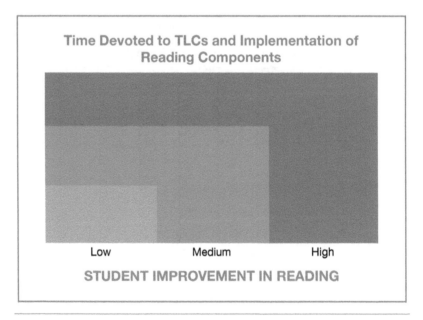

Source: Graphic by Leticia M. Trower

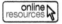 Available for download at http://resources.corwin.com/CMLExcellence

What Coaches Do for TLCs

▶ Motivate teachers to meet.

▶ Help develop an action plan for supporting MLs at beginning levels to build on their reading foundations.

▶ Help develop an action plan for supporting MLs at higher levels to move toward higher-complexity literacy skills.

▶ Help identify obstacles to successfully achieving personal and school goals.

▶ Start those sticky conversations about equity, bias, expectations, and dispositions.

▶ Remind teachers to build SEL into the reading lessons.

▶ Remind teachers to connect background knowledge, culturally relevant texts or topics, and ample interaction opportunities.

Coaches Can Help ESL and Content Teachers Work Together

MLs are no longer the responsibility of just the English as a second language (ESL) teachers—all teachers in middle and high schools share the responsibility for teaching their subject matter in a way that reaches all MLs in their classrooms. Mainstream teachers welcome and share their classroom for co-teaching with the ESL teachers.

ESL teachers are invited to attend TLCs by grade-level or content-area team meetings to help integrate ESL and subject curriculum programs. These critical relationships make a positive impact on the school while helping students reach their best social and academic outcomes.

Coaching is relationship building in a school. Nevertheless, coaching might bring to the forefront matters that often can't be addressed in merely coaching formats. The systems within and beyond the school need to be analyzed, followed by whole-school professional development that focuses attention on areas for change.

Hargreaves and Fullan (2012) noted the irony that "disagreement is more frequent in schools with collaborative cultures because purposes, values, and their relationships are always up for discussion" (p. 113). There will be disagreements and discomfort when the whole faculty begins discussions they have never had before about MLs. Yet, as Hargreaves and Fullan noted, "To manage the disagreement and risk are sources of dynamic group learning and improvement" (p. 111).

"People do not resist change; they resist being changed" (Dick Beckhard, quoted in Senge et al., 1999, p. 332).

Listening to Teachers' Voices

What is the nature of your relationship with teachers? First, you will want to establish trust by listening to their goals, hopes, fears, and choices in the coaching process. Second, remember that teachers already have a lot of knowledge about students and maybe even instructional strategies for teaching MLs. Third, make sure the teachers understand the school's plan for the coaching component. Leave a copy of the plan with every teacher. Fourth, discuss the options for the teachers and jointly adjust the plan while adhering to fidelity.

Type of Coaching. Do they prefer for you to help with a lesson plan first? For you to model the new strategies? Co-teach with you? Co-teach with the ESL teacher and you? Video the lesson for the coach?

Type of Observation. Observe for ten minutes only and give feedback. Observe students as they conduct the partner reading or vocabulary practice. Can a seating chart indicate which students to focus on?

Type or Mode of Feedback. How would the teacher like to receive the feedback—face-to-face, via email, in a Zoom meeting, or another way?

Coaches should jointly agree on a feedback protocol with their teachers. This will help both of you have an easy point of departure and to speak the same language. Sample conversation prompts for the feedback sessions are provided in Figure 6.6.

Figure 6.6   Conversation Prompts for the ML Coaches' Feedback Sessions

Thank you for letting me observe your lesson.

What did you think about your lesson?

What did you like best?

What did you observe in your students?

Here's the data I collected. What do you see?

Do you have any questions for me?

What goal would you set for your next lesson?

Be sure to celebrate successes!

Types of Discourse by the Coach to Delve Into Deeper Conversations.

- Tell me about your idea.
- What challenges are you facing?
- What do you need to be successful?
- How can I support that?
- How are you really doing? Feeling?
- I trust your judgment.
- You've got this.
- We've got this.
- I believe in you.

The Benefits of an Observation Protocol

Using an observation protocol makes coaching so much easier! It is extremely helpful in vulnerable situations such as multilingual classroom performance. All the observation protocols for vocabulary, reading, and writing strategies in Chapters 3, 4, and 5 were tested for validity and reliability. After using it for more than two decades with a few reiterations, my ExC-ELL coaches and I have found many benefits for teachers and coaches. The following are some comments teachers and coaches have shared with us.

- "An observation protocol helps us to be on the same page."
- "As a teacher, I can pick and choose where I need feedback."
- "As a coach, I know exactly what the teacher needs feedback on."
- "An observation protocol makes our conversations easier and saves us time."
- "As a coach, it helps me to communicate more effectively and not do a lot of bird walking or hedging like I did before."
- "I like getting a chance to reflect and share my views on my lesson before the coach starts to speak."
- "I like that the teacher answers 'How do you feel about your lesson?' before I talk."
- "From the reading menu, I know exactly what I need to work on next."
- "This simple process motivates me to keep on keeping on. It's easy!"
- "It is so much easier to reach agreement on a goal or next steps with the protocol."

Agreements and relationships between coaches and teachers are the significant features of a successful implementation of new learnings and their impact on student success. An objective but valid and reliable instrument will help ease tension or apprehension about coaching and feedback.

Coaching for Equity and Success

Going beyond conversations about equity, a school can begin to enact instructional support systems that will ensure equity for MLs and all students who will benefit from a quality implementation of the features described in this book. Whole-school reform can focus on establishing high academic standards and higher expectations while applying comprehensive instruction and participation in well-designed professional development systems, undergirded by greater accountability for adults and striving students.

The ExC-ELL development team and I began this work many years ago with an understanding of the social and emotional aspects of learning. We understood the importance of cultural knowledge, the ways variations in language and culture influence knowledge and learning, and how literacy itself and varied academic disciplines reflect specific social practices that students need to understand to be successful. In many ways, the field has been catching up with all of this over the decades.

Language and Literacy Across the Disciplines

Vocabulary and literacy are now understood to vary across academic disciplines. The role of social-emotional factors in learning is better understood, and SEL integrated into academic learning is seen as vital to student achievement. We also know more about how culture and socially shaped experiences build specific knowledge and personal agency in learning.

A Whole-School Approach Foundation

We know that administrators need to be fully involved in the implementation of a language, literacy, and content integration professional development and instructional approach. Administrators also need to know about coaching in multilingual settings. When they attend a workshop designed for them, they explore and answer critical questions and make a preliminary plan to take back to the teachers to discuss and where possible adapt, adopt, and implement.

Principals as Coaches

Why principals as coaches? The role of the principal as a coach is still controversial. Can a principal be a coach and an evaluator? Principals do play a major role by learning about and supporting ML coaching in all classrooms. They can make or break a quality-coaching implementation.

By inviting principals and assistant principals to join the teachers in their professional development sessions, coaches can acknowledge their value to the whole-school change effort. In follow-up sessions, principals and coaches discuss how to sustain a systematic coaching program. The principals and coaches should discuss the issue of transfer from training into the teachers' active teaching delivery and what happens "if and when" that transfers into student outcomes. Principals should also be encouraged to shadow coaches as they go from classroom to classroom to observe. Subsequently, they should join the debriefing of observations before moving to the next classroom. For the feedback sessions, principals should be invited only when teachers feel comfortable having them there. Principals will appreciate the experience and find the observation tools most valuable when they put on their hats as evaluators later in the year. Principals will also value the comprehensiveness of the professional learning approach as they are better able to see the micro aspects of teaching that make a difference.

Supovitz et al. (2010) found that school leadership leads to greater teacher and student success when principals draw attention to the school's mission and goals, strengthen trust in the school, and focus on instruction. Supovitz and colleagues found that principals who effectively lead a whole-staff coaching system are process experts and can lead the teachers on the path to accomplishing their goals.

What Coaches Do to Help Principals Map the Mission and Goals

A key message for principals is that professional development is most effective when it is delivered as part of a systematic, long-term approach to school, teacher, and student improvement. A new mindset and school ethos is necessary for everyone. The principal must strengthen the faculty's skills for conflict resolution and negotiation as they travel to unfamiliar territory.

Among the difficulties they will face is changing the habit of the one-shot workshop to sustained systematic learning. One-shot workshops remain a common form of professional development in many schools, even though participants report little meaningful change in their classroom practice (Garet et al., 2001). We have seen no benefits for MLs without sustained systematic professional learning. On the other hand, the two- and three-year commitments to continuous professional learning and coaching yield the type of changes that bring success to MLs, all students, and the school.

Most schools have instructional coaches and a preferred coaching model. We would like to invite you to consider adapting, adding, or deleting certain features to make room for a model inclusive of MLs. Figure 6.7 provides some discussion questions to guide the enactment of a multilingual/multicultural model of coaching.

Figure 6.7   Coaches Can Help Administrators Make Appropriate Changes on Coaching

FOR DISCUSSION	FOR ENACTMENT
Do your teachers understand the plans: the what, why, and how of coaching?	
Who are our coaches (e.g., experts, peers, co-teachers)?	
What are the coaches' roles and responsibilities?	
What actions can principals take to best support coaches?	
How will coaches use their time?	
Will observation data be anonymous? Desegregated?	
What is our goal this year for our coaches?	
What are the biggest barriers for a quality-coaching implementation?	
How might the whole school address those barriers?	

 Available for download at http://resources.corwin.com/CMLExcellence

Features of an Effective System for Whole-School Professional Learning

As the whole faculty and leadership move toward making changes, consider the following:

1. Delivering a clear, sequential teaching/learning methodology

2. Focusing on the components: language, discourse, literacy, SEL, cultural connections, and cooperative learning integrated into all subject areas

3. Incorporating research briefs and hands-on modeling and practice of the instructional strategies

4. Providing daily substantial opportunities for MLs to talk, listen to peers, read, process information, read some more, and write to bring it all together

5. Coaching teachers after each component is presented

6. Having coaches, teachers, administrators, librarians, counselors, and psychologists attend the workshops together

7. Scheduling and sustaining TLCs or other teacher collegial communities that focus on MLs

8. Enacting teacher support, accountability, and sustainability systems

9. Monitoring implementation and MLs' learning progressions, driving transformation

Coaching works when the whole school is prepared and fully informed about coaching and instruction that works in multilingual/multicultural schools. An ML-oriented whole-school approach is designed to embrace diversity, highlight MLs' assets, and help all educators in the school see not only how these talented students have been historically underserved and historically unrecognized but also that we must do something about it now (Calderón & Tartaglia, 2023). The whole-school approach works because it centers on MLs' development of skills that enable them to thrive in a new learning context, regulate emotions, navigate across cultures, and form healthy relationships. Plus, the whole school also benefits from recognition.

Ask teachers in TLCs and the leadership team in their meetings to map out their journey using the instructions provided in Figure 6.8 and the organizer provided in Figure 6.9.

Figure 6.8 Forecasting Transfer

- Draw the road on the poster page.
- Include hurdles, detours, and lifesavers.
- Add traffic lights or useful artifacts.
- Highlight the end-of-the-year splash.
- Label all the parts.
- Present to the school.

Figure 6.9 The Beginning of a Road Map for Principals: Fill in Blank Spaces

ENHANCING TEACHER CAPACITY	STRENGTHENING KNOWLEDGE, DISPOSITION, AND SKILLS	PROFESSIONAL DEVELOPMENT (THROUGH THEORY, RESEARCH, MODELING, AND PRACTICE)	EFFECTIVE INSTRUCTIONAL PRACTICE
		• Analyzing texts to select vocabulary and syntax MLs might need	
		• Teaching vocabulary and discourse	
		• Modeling reading comprehension skills	
		• Teaching reading comprehension	
		• Social-emotional learning	
		• Social-cultural teaching and learning	
		• Working and learning with peers	
		• Writing in each content area: drafting, editing, revising	
		• Appropriate assessments	

 Available for download at http://resources.corwin.com/CMLExcellence

As mentioned in Chapter 1, very few studies of coaching serve to guide implementation for interested schools. We need more descriptive, qualitative, and quantitative studies in multilingual schools to validate coaching, showcase successes, and gain broader support for coaching. I invite you to conduct a study as you implement your program.

Begin by documenting how coaches of teachers with multilingual/ multicultural students strengthen quality instruction and sustain it throughout the year. By anchoring the multilingual/multicultural coaching model in Jim Knight's (2022) seven success factors, as shown in Figure 6.10, we can see that these models align.

Figure 6.10   Parallels With Jim Knight's (2022) Seven Success Factors

1.	**Partnership principles**	The multilingual coach builds relationships with teachers, administrators, multilingual students, and their families.
2.	**Communication skills**	The multilingual coach combines the language of coaching focused on professional growth and the language of multilingual multiliteracies and effective instructional practices (e.g., vocabulary, discourse, reading, writing, SEL, cooperative learning, and the writing process).
3.	**Coaches as leaders**	The multilingual coach is a powerful leader and advocate for multilingual learners' and their teachers' success.
4.	**The impact cycle**	The multilingual coach uses a variety of coaching structures to facilitate a teacher's preference for learning.
5.	**Data**	The multilingual coach collects data on the specific observation/feedback protocols to focus on student and teacher learning progressions.
6.	**The instructional playbook**	The playbook components described in Chapters 3, 4, and 5 are the high-impact teaching strategies that the multilingual coaches can use to partner with teachers so they and their students can meet their goals.
7.	**System support**	The multilingual coach is supported by leadership and plays a crucial role in implementing new ways of teaching, new ways of thinking about MLs, and sustainability of success for all.

Schools that are serious about helping MLs succeed academically can begin their journey by creating success for coaches and teachers. I wrote this book to share evidence-based components that work when implemented systematically as seen in many schools already. My goal is to make the transfer into the teachers' active teaching repertoire as easy as possible, empowered by their coaches as they study this book and transfer that learning into their coaching repertoire to impact instruction and MLs' academic success.

Wishing everyone great success!

Message From a Special Guest: Ongoing Professional Development

By Karen Johannesen Brock

An instructional coach can be an asset to a school in a variety of ways. The instructional coach is focused on implementation at the classroom level and deepens the implementation of

- The school's professional learning plan
- Curriculum
- District initiatives
- PLCs

As an educational consultant and writer (*Coaching for Multilingual Student Success: Intentional Practices to Accelerate Learning and Close Achievement Gaps*, 2024), I have worked with more than 150 schools and have come to know the power of instructional coaching as a vehicle to support rapid and sustainable change in instructional practice and student outcomes. Instructional coaching is most productive when it is tied to the implementation of an ongoing professional learning plan.

Ongoing = 4 or more sessions with clearly articulated implementation outcomes.

All of the teachers in the school will take part in ongoing professional learning that is tied to the focus topic. Training sessions include theory, demonstration, and opportunities for practice and lesson planning. At the conclusion of each session, the principal summarizes the work completed in the session, indicates the goals of the upcoming session, and gives all teachers an implementation assignment to be completed between sessions. The instructional coach works with each teacher on the implementation assignment. When coaches are part of the implementation plan of a school improvement goal, every classroom moves quickly toward implementation. The coach will set individual goals with each teacher—thus personalizing the implementation assignment to the unique teacher strengths and honoring the complexity of each classroom.

What	Learn: theory, demonstration, practice, lesson planning	Assignment: e.g., in the 6 weeks between sessions, utilize the strategy at least 15 times	Coaching: e.g., in the science teacher's class, the coach co-plans 4 lessons with the teacher utilizing the strategy
Who	All teachers, administrators, instructional coaches	All teachers	All teachers

Coaching is embedded into the work of the school, and professional learning goals are implemented into every classroom within weeks. As an example, if a school has decided to implement a close reading process that includes vocabulary instruction and partner feedback, the teachers are introduced to the process in a professional learning session. They leave the session with an understanding of the theory and the research behind close reading and vocabulary instruction, having watched video examples of the process in a classroom and practiced lesson planning. Teachers are asked to plan and implement a close reading process three times a week over the following six weeks. The instructional coach works with each teacher and will offer a variety of options such as support for lesson planning, co-teaching, modeling, taking engagement data, and debriefing. This personalized process is repeated across the school. At the end of six weeks, teachers have practiced a close reading routine several times and have intentionally aligned this process with the curricular goals of the classroom. At that time, they are ready to begin the next step of the professional learning plan. The most important benefit is the assurance that every student has participated in this process multiple times and has measurably increased reading proficiency, vocabulary, and dialogue skill within a few weeks.

Karen Johannesen Brock, PhD, is the director of professional development and instructional coaching for the Provo (Utah) School District.

References

Abreu, Y. (2011). How a middle school went from reconstituted to highest performing in two years: A principal's perspective. In M. Calderón & L. Minaya-Rowe (pp. 119–130). *Preventing long-term ELs: Transforming schools to meet core standards*. Corwin.

Aguilar, E. (2013). *The art of coaching: Effective strategies for school transformation*. Jossey-Bass.

Aguilar, E. (2014, May 1). Effective coaching by design. *Educational Leadership, 71*(8). ASCD. https://www.ascd.org/el/articles/effective-coaching-by-design

Aguilar, E. (2016). *The art of coaching teams: Building resilient communities that transform schools*. Jossey-Bass.

Aguilar, E. (2018). *Onward: Cultivating emotional resilience in educators*. Wiley.

Aguilar, E. (2020). *Coaching for equity: Conversations that change practice*. Jossey-Bass.

Archibald, S., Coggshall, J. G., Croft, A., & Goe, L. (2011). *High-quality professional development for all teachers: Effectively allocating resources*. National Comprehensive Center for Teacher Quality. https://files.eric.ed.gov/fulltext/ED520732.pdf

Armstrong, P. (2010). *Bloom's taxonomy*. Vanderbilt University Center for Teaching. https://cft.vanderbilt.edu/guides-sub-pages/blooms-taxonomy/

Artzi, L., August, D., & Gray, J. L. (2019). Fostering English learners' academic language in a science-themed summer school program. In P. Spycher & E. F. Haynes (Eds.), *Culturally and linguistically diverse learners and STEAM: Teachers and researchers working in partnership to build a better tomorrow* (pp. 27–44). Information Age.

August, D., Barr, C., Carlson, C., Cardenas-Hagan, E., Johnston, W. T., & Marken, A. (2023). A promising intervention designed to improve EAL learners' mathematics skills and associated academic language. *Bilingual Research Journal, 46*(1–2), 117–141. https://doi.org/10.1080/1523588 2.2023.2225459

August, D., Beck, I. L., Calderón, M., Francis, D. J., Lesaux, N. K., & Shanahan, T. (2008). Instruction and professional development. In D. August & T. Shanahan (Eds.), *Developing reading and writing in second language learners: Lessons from the Report of the National Literacy Panel on Language-Minority Children and Youth* (pp. 131–250). Lawrence Erlbaum Associates.

August, D., Calderón, M., & Carlo, M. (2001). Transfer of reading skills from Spanish to English: A study of young learners. *National Association for Bilingual Education Journal, 24*(4), 11–42.

August, D., Carlo, M., Dressler, C., & Snow, C. (2005, January 11). The critical role of vocabulary development for English language learners. *Learning Disabilities Research & Practice, 20*(1), 50–57. https://doi.org/10.1111/j.1540-5826.2005.00120.x

August, D., & Shanahan, T. (Eds.). (2006). *Developing literacy in second-language learners: Report of the National Literacy Panel on Language-Minority Children and Youth*. Lawrence Erlbaum Associates.

August, D., & Shanahan, T. (Eds.). (2008). *Developing reading and writing in second-language learners: Lessons from the report of the National Literacy Panel on Language-Minority Children and Youth*. Lawrence Erlbaum Associates.

Barth, R. (1990). *Improving schools from within: Teachers, parents, and principals can make a difference*. Jossey-Bass.

Batalova, J. (2024, March 13). *Frequently requested statistics on immigrants and immigration in the United States*. Migration Policy Institute. https://www.migrationpolicy.org/article/frequently-requested-statistics-immigrants-and-immigration-united-states-2024

Beck, I. L., McKeown, G., & Kucan, L. (2005). Choosing words to teach. In E. H. Hiebert & M. L. Kamil (Eds.), *Teaching and learning vocabulary: Bringing research to practice* (pp. 207–222). Lawrence Erlbaum Associates.

Bright Morning. (2024). *Are you ready to transform your school?* https://www.brightmorningteam.com/

Brock, K. J. (2023). *Coaching for multilingual success: Improving student learning through instructional coaching.* Solution Tree.

Brown, D., Reumann-Moore, R., Hugh, R., du Plessis, P., & Christman, J. B. (2006). *Promising inroads: Year one report of the Pennsylvania High School Coaching Initiative.* Research for Action.

Buenrostro, M., & Maxwell-Jolly, J. (2021). *Renewing our promise: Research and recommendations to support California's long-term English learners.* Californians Together.

Calderón, M. E. (1984). *Training bilingual trainers: A quantitative and ethnographic study of coaching and its impact on the transfer of training* [Doctoral dissertation]. Claremont Graduate University/San Diego State University.

Calderón, M. (1984, 1986, 1990, 1994, 1996). *Sheltered instruction: Manual for teachers and teacher trainers.* ExC-ELL.

Calderón, M. (1991). Cooperative learning builds communities of teachers. *Journal of Teacher Education and Practice, 6*(2), 75–79.

Calderón, M. (1995). *Cooperative learning for secondary schools: Manual for teachers and teacher trainers.* MTTI.

Calderón, M. (1999). Teachers learning communities for cooperation in diverse settings. *Theory Into Practice, 38*(2), 94–99.

Calderón, M. E. (2007). *Teaching reading to English language learners, Grades 6–12: A framework for improving achievement in the content areas.* Corwin.

Calderón, M. E. (2011). *Teaching reading and comprehension to English learners, K–5.* Solution Tree Press.

Calderón, M. E. (2016). A whole-school approach to English learners. *Educational Leadership, 73*(5). ASCD.

Calderón, M. E. (2020). Getting newcomers into the academic flow. *Educational Leadership, 77*(4), 68–73.

Calderón, M. E. (2022). *ExC-ELL manual* (5th ed.). Margarita Calderón & Associates, Inc.

Calderón, M., August, D., Slavin, R., Cheung, A., Durán, D., & Madden, N. (2005). Bringing words to life in classrooms with English language learners. In E. H. Hiebert & M. L. Kamil (Eds.), *Teaching and learning vocabulary: Bringing research to practice* (pp. 115–136). Lawrence Erlbaum Associates.

Calderón, M., & Carreón, A. (1994). Educators and students use cooperative learning to become biliterate and bilingual. *Cooperative Learning, 14*(3), 6–9.

Calderón, M., & Carreón, A. (2001). A dual language bilingual program: Promise, practice and precautions. In R. E. Slavin & M. Calderón (Eds.), *Effective programs for Latino students* (pp. 125–170). Lawrence Erlbaum Associates.

Calderón, M. E., Espino, G., & Slakk, S. (2019). *Integrando lenguaje, lectura, escritura y contenidos en español e inglés/Integrating language, reading, writing and content in English and Spanish.* Velàzquez Press.

Calderón, M. E., Hertz-Lazarowitz, R., & Slavin, R. E. (1998). Effects of bilingual cooperative integrated reading and composition on students making the transition from Spanish to English reading. *The Elementary School Journal, 99*(2). http://www.journals.uchicago.edu/doi/abs/10.1086/461920; https://ies.ed.gov/ncee/wwc/EvidenceSnapshot/47

Calderón, M., & Marsh, D. (1989). Applying research on effective bilingual instruction in a multi-district inservice teacher training program. *National Association for Bilingual Education, 12*(2), 133–152.

Calderón, M. E., & Minaya-Rowe, L. (2003). *Designing and implementing two-way bilingual programs: A step-by step guide for administrators, teachers, and parents.* Corwin.

Calderón, M. E., & Minaya-Rowe, L. (2011). *Preventing long-term English language learners: Transforming schools to meet core standards.* Corwin.

Calderón, M., & Montenegro, H. (2021). *Empowering long-term ELs with social emotional learning, language, literacy, and content.* Velázquez Press.

Calderón, M. E., Slavin, R. E., & Sánchez, M. (2011). Effective instruction for English language learners. In M. Tienda & R. Haskins (Eds.), *The future of immigrant children.* Brookings Institution/Princeton University. http://www.futureofchildren.org/futureof children/publications/docs/21_01_05.pdf

Calderón, M., & Spiegel-Coleman, S. (1985). Effective instruction for language minority students—from theory to practice. *Teacher Education Journal, 2*(3).

Calderon, M. E., & Tartaglia, L. M. (with Montenegro, H.). (2023). *Cultivating competence in English learners: Integrating social-emotional learning with language and literacy.* Solution Tree.

Calderón, M. E., Trower, L. M., Tartaglia, L., M., & Montenegro, H. (2022). *Expediting comprehension for English learners (ExC- ELL) teachers manual* (9th ed.). Margarita Calderón & Associates, Inc.

California State Department of Education. (Ed.). (1981). *Schooling and language minority students: A theoretical framework* (pp. 3–50). California State University.

Calkins, L. (2017). *A guide to the writing workshop: Primary grades.* Heinemann.

Carhill, A., Suarez-Orozco, C., & Paez, M. (2008). Explaining English language proficiency among adolescent immigrant students. *American Educational Research Journal, 45*(4), 1155–1179. https://www .jstor.org/stable/27667165

Cashiola, L., & Potter, D. (2020). *Long-term English learners (LTELs): Predictors, patterns, and outcomes.* Brief 1: Defining LTEL. Houston Education Research Consortium, Kinder Institute for Urban Research, Rice University.

Chall, J. S. (1996). American reading achievement: Should we worry? *Research in the Teaching of English, 30*(3), 303–310. https://www.jstor.org/stable/40171366

Collaborative for Academic, Social, and Emotional Learning. (n.d.). *Fundamentals of SEL.* https://casel.org/fundamentals-of-sel/

Costa, A. L., & Garmston, R. J. (2015). *Cognitive coaching: Developing self-directed leaders and learners* (3rd ed.). Rowman & Littlefield.

Darling-Hammond, L., & McLaughlin, M. W. (1995). Policies that support professional development in an era of reform. *Phi Delta Kappan, 76*(8), 597–604.

Darling-Hammond, L., & Richardson, N. (2009). Research review/teacher learning: What matters? *Educational Leadership, 66*(5). https://www.ascd.org/el/articles/ teacher-learning-what-matters

Dawson, P., & Guare, R. (2018). *Executive skills in children and adolescents: A practical guide to assessment and intervention.* Guilford Press.

Delpit, L. (1995). *Other people's children: Cultural conflict in the classroom.* Norton.

DeWitt, P. (2023, June 8). Want to strengthen leadership coaching? Try collaborative inquiry. *EducationWeek.* https:// www.edweek.org/leadership/opinion- want-to-strengthen-leadership-coaching- try-collaborative-inquiry/2023/06

Diamond, A. (2013). Executive functions. *Annual Review of Psychology, 64*(1), 135–168. http://doi.org/10.1146/annurev-psych- 113011-143750

Dougherty, J. (2021). Translanguaging in action: Pedagogy that elevates. *ORTESOL Journal, 38,* 19–31. https://files.eric .ed.gov/fulltext/EJ1305313.pdf

DuFour, R., & DuFour, R. (2012). *The school leader's guide to professional learning communities at work.* Solution Tree.

Duke, N. K., Ward, A. E., & Pearson, P. D. (2021). The science of reading comprehension instruction. *The Reading Teacher, 74*(6), 663–672. https://doi.org/10.1002/ trtr.1993

Edwards, J. (2024). *Cognitive Coaching[SM]: A synthesis of the research* (18th ed.). Thinking Collaborative. https://www .thinkingcollaborative.com/_files/ugd/ d00b6c_63cc661d4b274d51baf233ed- 1bc6c470.pdf

Ehri, L. C. (2014). Orthographic mapping in the acquisition of sight word reading, spelling memory, and vocabulary learning.

Scientific Studies of Reading, 18(1), 5–21. http://doi.org/10.1080/10888438.2013.8 19356

Environmental Protection Agency. (2024, January 2). *Climate change impacts: Climate equity.* https://www.epa.gov/climateimpacts/climate-equity

Fullan, M. (2001). *Leading in a culture of change.* Jossey-Bass.

Garet, M. S., Porter, A. C., Desimone, L., Birman, B. F., & Yoon, K. S. (2001). What makes professional development effective? Results from a national sample of teachers. *American Educational Research Journal, 38*(4), 915–945. https://doi.org/10.3102/00028312038004915

Goodman, K. S. (1992). *The whole language catalog: Supplement on authentic assessment.* American School Publishers.

Gottlieb, M., & Calderon, M. E. (in press). *Together we can! ¡Juntos podemos! Modules.* Velazquez Press.

Graham, S., & Alves, R. A. (2021). Research and teaching writing. *Reading and Writing, 34,* 1613–1621. https://doi.org/10.1007/s11145-021-10188-9

Graham, S., Camping, A., Harris, K., Aitken, A. A., Wilson, J. M., Wdowin, J., & Ng, C. (2021). Writing and writing motivation of students identified as English language learners. *International Journal of TESOL Studies, 3*(1), 1–13. https://doi.org/10.46451/ijts.2021.01.01

Graham, S., & Hebert, M. A. (2010). *Writing to read: Evidence for how writing can improve reading. A Carnegie Corporation Time to Act Report.* Alliance for Excellent Education.

Graham, S., & Hebert, M. (2011). Writing to read: A meta-analysis of the impact of writing and writing instruction on reading. *Harvard Educational Review, 81*(4), 710–744. http://www.metapress.com/content/t2kom13756113566/?p=b750fb72579a4bf-888463053ba9df9b9&pi=4

Graham, S., & Perin, D. (2007). *Writing next: Effective strategies to improve writng of adolescents in middle and high schools.* Carnegie Corporation of New York.

Graves, M., August, D., & Carlo, M. (2011). Teaching 50,000 words. *Better, 3*(2), 6–7.

Guilamo, A. (2022, July 13). The science of the bilingual reading brain. *Language Magazine.* https://www.languagemagazine.com/2022/07/13/the-science-of-the-bilingual-reading-brain/

Guskey, T. R. (1997). Research needs to link professional development and student learning. *Journal of Staff Development, 18*(2), 36–40.

Hargreaves, A., & Fullan, M. (2012). *Professional capital: Transforming teaching in every school.* Teachers College Press.

Hattie, J. (2009). *Visible learning: A synthesis of over 800 meta-analyses relating to achievement.* Routledge.

Hattie, J. (2012). *Visible learning for teachers: Maximizing impact on learning.* Routledge.

Hattie, J., & Clarke, S. (2019). *Visible learning feedback.* Routledge.

Hattie, J., & Timperley, H. (2007). The power of feedback. *American Educational Research Association, 77*(1), 81–112. https://doi.org/10.3102/003465430298487

Hattie, J., & Yates, G. (2014). *Visible learning and the science of how we learn.* Routledge.

Hertz-Lazarowitz, R., Sharan, S., & Steinberg, R. (1980). Classroom learning style and cooperative behavior of elementary school children. *Journal of Educational Psychology, 72*(1), 99–106. https://doi.org/10.1037/0022-0663.72.1.99

Hiebert, E. H., & Kamil, M. L. (Eds.). (2005). *Teaching and learning vocabulary: Bringing research to practice.* Lawrence Erlbaum Associates.

Hill, H. C., Litke, E., & Lynch, K. (2018). Learning lessons from instruction: Descriptive results from an observational study of urban elementary classrooms. *Teachers' College Record, 120*(12), 1–46. https://dash.harvard.edu/handle/1/37366148

Honigsfeld, A., Dove, M. G., Cohan, A., & Goldman, C. M. (2022). *From equity insights to action: Critical strategies for teaching multilingual learners.* Corwin Press.

Howard, E. R., Lindholm-Leary, K. J., Rogers, D., Olague, N., Medina, J., Kennedy, B., Sugarman, J., & Christian, D. (2018). *Guiding principles for dual language education* (3rd ed.). Center for Applied Linguistics.

Instructional Coaching Group. (n.d.). *The instructional coaching blog.* https://www.instructionalcoaching.com/blog

Joyce, B. R., & Showers, B. (1982a). The coaching of teaching. *Educational Leadership, 40*(1), 4–10.

Joyce, B. R., & Showers, B. (1982b). Transfer of training: The contribution of "coaching." *Journal of Education, 163*(2), 163–172.

Joyce, B. R., & Showers, B. (2002). *Student achievement through staff development* (3rd ed.). Association for Supervision and Curriculum Development.

Joyce, B. R., & Weil, M. (1980). *Models of teaching* (2nd ed). Prentice-Hall.

Kee, K., Anderson, K., Dearing, V., Harris, E., & Shuster, F. (2010). *Results coaching: The new essential for school leaders.* Corwin.

Kelcey, B., Hill, H. C., & Chin, M. J. (2019). Teacher mathematical knowledge, instructional quality, and student outcomes: A multilevel quantile mediation analysis. *School Effectiveness and School Improvement, 30*(4), 398–431. https://doi.org/10.1080/09243453.2019.1570944

Killion, J., Bryan, C., & Clifton, H. (2020). *Coaching matters* (2nd ed.). Learning Forward.

Knight, J. (2007). *Instructional coaching: A partnership approach for improving instruction.* Corwin.

Knight, J. (2018). *The impact cycle: What instructional coaches should do to foster powerful improvements in teaching.* Corwin.

Knight, J. (2019). Instructional coaching for implementing visible learning: A model for translating research into practice. *Education Sciences, 9*(2), Article 101. https://doi.org/10.3390/educsci9020101

Knight, J. (2021, February 1). Moving from talk to action in professional learning. *Educational Leadership, 78*(5). ASCD.

https://www.ascd.org/el/articles/moving-from-talk-to-action-in-professional-learning

Knight, J. (2022). *The definitive guide to instructional coaching: Seven factors for success.* ASCD.

Knight, J. (2023). [Preconference workshop.] ASCD Annual Conference.

Knight, J., Hoffman, A., Harris, M., & Thomas, S. (2020). *The instructional playbook: The missing link for translating research into practice.* ASCD.

Kraft, M. K., & Hill, H. C. (2020). Developing ambitious mathematics instruction through web-based coaching: A randomized field trial. *American Educational Research Journal, 57*(6), 2378–2414. https://scholar.harvard.edu/mkraft/publications/developing-ambitious-mathematics-instruction-through-web-based-coaching

Lieberman, A. (1995). Practices that support teacher development. *Phi Delta Kappan, 76*(8), 591–596.

Little, J. W. (1990). The persistence of privacy: Autonomy and initiative in teachers' professional relations. *Teachers College Record, 91*(4), 509–536.

Lobosco, K. (2023, August 27). Schools got $190 billion in pandemic aid, but the funds haven't reversed learning loss. *CNN.* https://www.cnn.com/2023/08/27/politics/school-covid-pandemic-aid-learning-loss/index.html

Mahken, K. (2024, January 16). Amid literacy push, many states still don't prepare teachers for success, report finds. *The74.* https://www.the74million.org/article/amid-literacy-push-many-states-still-dont-prepare-teachers-for-success-report-finds/

Moats, L. C. (2020). *Teaching reading is rocket science, 2020: What expert teachers of reading should know and be able to do.* American Federation of Teachers. https://www.aft.org/sites/default/files/moats.pdf

National Academies of Sciences, Engineering, and Medicine. (2017). *Promoting the educational success of children and youth learning English: Promising futures.* The National Academies Press.

National Center for Education Statistics. (2023). *The condition of education 2023* (NCES 2023-144). Institute of Education Sciences, U.S. Department of Education. https://nces.ed.gov/pubs2023/2023144.pdf

National Center for Education Statistics. (2024). *English learners in public schools.* https://nces.ed.gov/programs/coe/indicator/cgf

National Reading Panel. (2000). *Teaching children to read: An evidence-based assessment of the scientific research literature on reading and its implications for reading instruction.* National Institute of Child Health and Human Development.

National Research Council. (2010). *Preparing teachers: Building evidence for sound policy. Report from the Committee on the Study of Teacher Preparation Programs in the United States.* National Academies Press.

Olsen, L. (2010). *Reparable harm: Fulfilling the unkept promise of educational opportunity for California's long term English learners.* Californians Together.

Olsen, L. (2014). *Meeting the unique needs of long-term English learners: A guide for educators.* National Education Association.

Palincsar, A. S., & Brown, A. L. (1984). Reciprocal teaching of comprehension fostering and comprehension monitoring activities. *Cognition and Instruction, 2,* 117–175.

Perfetti, C. A. (1985). *Reading ability.* Oxford University Press.

Regional Educational Laboratory West. (2016, November). *Long-term English learner students: Spotlight on an overlooked population.* WestEd. https://www.wested.org/wp-content/uploads/2016/11/LTEL-factsheet.pdf

Salmerón, L., Vargas, C., Delgado, P., & Baron, N. (2023). Relation between digital tool practices in the language arts classroom and reading comprehension scores. *Reading and Writing, 36*(6), 175–194. http://doi.org/10.1007/s11145-022-10295-1

Sawchuk, S. (2023, December 21). The stories that stuck with us. *EdWeek.* https://www.edweek.org/education/the-stories-that-stuck-with-us-2023-edition/2023/12

Schwartz, S. (2023, September 5). Teachers College to "dissolve" Lucy Calkins' reading and writing project. *Education Week.* https://www.edweek.org/teaching-learning/teachers-college-to-dissolve-lucy-calkins-reading-and-writing-project/2023/09

Seals, V. (2021, September). Benefits of translanguaging pedagogy and practice. *Scottish Languages Review, 36,* 1–8. https://www.researchgate.net/publication/354616492_Benefits_of_Translanguaging_Pedagogy_and_Practice

Senge, P., Kleiner, A., Roberts, C., Ross, R., Roth, G., & Smith, B. (1999). *The dance of change: The challenges of sustaining momentum in learning organizations.* Doubleday.

Shanahan, T. (2005). *The National Reading Panel report: Practical advice for teachers.* Learning Point Associates.

Shanahan, T. (2023a, August 5). Is digital text a good idea for reading instruction? *Shanahan on Literacy.* https://www.shanahanonliteracy.com/blog/is-digital-text-a-good-idea-for-reading-instruction

Shanahan, T. (2023b, July 22). Knowledge or comprehension strategies – What should we teach? *Shanahan on Literacy.* https://www.shanahanonliteracy.com/blog/knowledge-or-comprehension-strategies-what-should-we-teach

Shanahan, T. (2024a, January 13). What does brain science have to say about teaching reading? Does it matter? *Shanahan on Literacy.* https://www.shanahanonliteracy.com/blog/what-does-brain-science-have-to-say-about-teaching-reading-does-it-matter

Shanahan, T. (2024b, January 20). Blast from the past: How can we take advantage of the reading-writing relationship? *Shanahan on Literacy.* https://www.shanahanonliteracy.com/blog/blast-from-the-past-how-can-we-take-advantage-of-the-reading-writing-relationship

Short, D. J., & Fitzsimmons, S. (2007). *Double the work: Challenges and solutions to acquiring language and academic literacy for adolescent English language learners.* Alliance for Excellent Education.

Showers, B., Joyce, B., & Hertz-Lazarowitz, R. (1980). *Presentations at the Multidistrict Trainer of Trainers Institute (MTTI) training workshops*. Riverside, CA.

Slavin, R. E. (1975). *Classroom reward structure: Effects on academic performance, social connectedness, and peer norms*. [Unpublished doctoral dissertation]. Johns Hopkins University.

Slavin, R. E., & Calderón, M. (Eds.). (2001). *Effective programs for Latino students*. Lawrence Erlbaum Associates.

Slavin, R. E., & Madden, N. A. (2001). *One million children: Success for all*. Corwin.

Soto, I., Snyder, S., Calderón, M. E., Gottlieb, M., Honigsfeld, A., Lachance, J., Marshal, M., Nungaray, D., Flores, R., & Scott, L. (2024). *Breaking down the monolingual wall: Essential shifts for multilingual learners' success*. Corwin.

Sugarman, J. (2023, April). *Unlocking opportunities: Supporting English learners' equitable access to career and technical education*. Migration Policy Institute. https://www.migrationpolicy.org/

Supovitz, J., Sirinides, P., & May, H. (2010). How principals and peers influence teaching and learning. *Educational Administration Quarterly, 46*(1), 31–56. http://doi.org/10.1177/1094670509353043

Teemant, A., & Sherman, B. (2022). Agency, identity, power: An agentive triad model for teacher action. *Educational Philosophy and Theory, 54*(9), 1464–1475.

Tharp, R. G., & Gallimore, R. (1988). *Rousing minds to life: Teaching, learning, and schooling in social context*. Cambridge University Press.

The Reading League & National Committee for Effective Literacy. (2023). *Joint statement: Understanding the difference: The science of reading and implementation for English learners/emergent bilinguals (ELs/EBs)*. https://www.thereadingleague.org/wp-content/uploads/2023/10/Joint-Statement-on-the-Science-of-Reading-and-English-Learners_Emergent-Bilinguals-20.pdf

Umansky, I., & Reardon, S. F. (2014). Reclassification patterns among Latino English learner students in bilingual, dual immersion, and English immersion classrooms. *American Educational Research Journal, 51*, 879–912. https://doi.org/10.3102/0002831214545110

U.S. Department of Education & Office of English Language Acquisition. (2023). *Raising the bar for English learners: Tips and resources to create robust pathways to multilingualism* [Brochure]. https://ncela.ed.gov/sites/default/files/2024-03/multilingualisminfo-20231121-508-compressed.pdf

U.S. Department of Justice Civil Rights Division & U.S. Department of Education Office for Civil Rights. (2015, January 7). *Dear colleague letter: English learner students and limited English proficient parents*. https://www2.ed.gov/about/offices/list/ocr/letters/colleague-el-201501.pdf

U.S. Department of Justice Civil Rights Division & U.S. Department of Education Office for Civil Rights. (2023, June). *Protecting access to education for migratory children: A resource for families and educators* [Brochure]. https://www2.ed.gov/about/offices/list/ocr/docs/ocr-factsheet-unac companied-children-202306.pdf

Vaughn, S., Gersten, R., Dimino, J., Taylor, M. J., Newman-Gonchar, R., Krowka, S., Kieffer, M. J., McKeown, M., Reed, D., Sanchez, M., St. Martin, K., Wexler, J., Morgan, S., Yañez, A., & Jayanthi, M. (2022). *Providing reading interventions for students in grades 4–9* (WWC 2022007). National Center for Education Evaluation and Regional Assistance (NCEE), Institute of Education Sciences, U.S. Department of Education. https://ies.ed.gov/ncee/WWC/Docs/PracticeGuide/WWC-practice-guide-reading-intervention-full-text.pdf

WIDA. (2020). *WIDA English language development standards framework, 2020 edition: Kindergarten–grade 12*. Board of Regents of the University of Wisconsin System.

Williams, C. P. (2023, November 16). *America's missing bilingual teachers*. The Century Foundation. https://tcf

.org/content/commentary/americas-missing-bilingual-teachers/

Woulfin, S. L., & Jones, B. (2018). Rooted in relationships: An analysis of dimensions of social capital enabling instructional coaching. *Journal of Professional Capital and Community, 3*(1), 25–38. http://doi.org/10.1108/JPCC-07-2017-0017

Zacarian, D., Calderón, M. E., & Gottlieb, M. (2021). *Beyond crises: Overcoming linguistic and cultural inequities in communities, schools, and classrooms.* Corwin.

Index

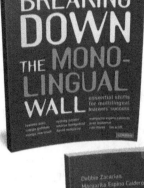

A Sage Company

CORWIN HAS ONE MISSION: to enhance education through intentional professional learning.

We build long-term relationships with our authors, educators, clients, and associations who partner with us to develop and continuously improve the best evidence-based practices that establish and support lifelong learning.